# How to Save The Dying Church of Christ

*Elevate Jesus*

*Above Tradition*

Daniel B. Lyle, Ph.D.

**LylePublishing**

Sulphur, Oklahoma

**How to Save the Dying Church of Christ**
*Elevate Jesus Above Tradition*
Copyright © 2014 by Daniel Basil Lyle

All rights reserved. No part of this book may be reproduced or transmitted in any form or by any means without written permission from the author, except in the case of brief quotations embodied in critical reviews and certain other noncommercial or educational uses permitted by copyright law. For permission requests, or any other questions, please send an e-mail to the author at the following address: DanLyle@LylePublishing.com.

ISBN 978-0-9794101-3-0

Published by LylePublishing
505 W. 12th Street, Sulphur, OK 73086
(www.LylePublishing.com)

Printed by CreateSpace, An Amazon.com company. Available from Amazon.com and other retail outlets. Also available as an ebook on Kindle and other devices.

## PREFACE

What do you want?  Do you want for your congregation to retain its young people once they grow up?  Do you want visitors to be intrigued enough to return?  Do you want your membership inspired and excited about attending church?  Do you want an effective local evangelistic effort that actually brings in new people?  Do you want your community to be impressed with your presence?  Or, conversely, do you wish to honor your traditional beliefs and practices above all else---even if they no longer connect with your present day society?  Do you wish to demonize anyone "doing church" different from you?  Do you want to become an isolated, ingrown, and dwindling club of God's "true believers"?  Do you want to ignore what truly works for bringing people to God in order to repeat, for yet one more time, boring rituals?  If you prefer the first set of objectives I've listed above, then I offer strong advice that might set you on the path to achieving those desired results!  Yes, this book is, indeed, a "slap in the face" to those who *ignore* results to deify methods.  It places Jesus' Radical Principles above all else, including cherished procedures.  But I offer not just harsh criticism.  I also give you many practical, workable Action Items to consider for revitalizing your congregation and moving your people ever-closer to God.  But it all rests on the one simple question: "What do you want?"

*Dan Lyle, 7-9-2014*

## TABLE OF CONTENTS

*Preface* . . . . . . . . . . . . . . . . . . . . . . . . . . . . . . . . . . . . . . . . . . 3

*Introduction* . . . . . . . . . . . . . . . . . . . . . . . . . . . . . . . . . . . . 5

CHAPTER:

1. **The Worship Service** . . . . . . . . . . . . . . . . . . . . . . . 11
2. **Group Meetings** . . . . . . . . . . . . . . . . . . . . . . . . . . . 29
3. **Doctrine** . . . . . . . . . . . . . . . . . . . . . . . . . . . . . . . . . . . 51
4. **Evangelism** . . . . . . . . . . . . . . . . . . . . . . . . . . . . . . . 67
5. **Church Management** . . . . . . . . . . . . . . . . . . . . . . 97
6. **Church Leadership** . . . . . . . . . . . . . . . . . . . . . . . 141
7. **Crisis Management** . . . . . . . . . . . . . . . . . . . . . . . 169

*Conclusion* . . . . . . . . . . . . . . . . . . . . . . . . . . . . . . . . . . . 195

*About the Author* . . . . . . . . . . . . . . . . . . . . . . . . . . . . . 197

*Other Books by Dr. Lyle* . . . . . . . . . . . . . . . . . . . . . . 198

-------------------------------------------------

# Introduction:

The protestant Christian denomination calling itself "The Church of Christ" is dying. Although there do exist some notable exceptions, most Church of Christ congregations are steadily shrinking. This decline has been occurring for decades and is presently accelerating. Along with dwindling numbers of members within congregations, the average age of the membership is also steadily increasing. Memberships are now often gray or white-haired with few if any children present.

This decades-long steady loss of membership is directly due to three factors: 1) the drifting away of existing members, 2) lack of effective evangelism to recruit new members, and--- most troubling of all--- 3) failure to retain the members' own maturing children.

As a life-long, faithful member of this group for more than 65 years, plus being an author of several books on Quality Management (see LylePublishing.com) I feel I have a unique perspective to offer suggestions for possibly stopping and reversing this sad decline. I have directly observed all the problems I discuss in this short book, feel great sympathy for the people caught in these ungodly situations (both for the "regular" members and the church leaders), and am willing to put my own "neck on the line" to point out these large problems.

But I'm not just criticizing. I'm also offering many solutions that are practical and helpful---should there be a willingness to do better for Jesus and move ever-closer to God.

Note that I am not claiming that Christianity as a religion is dying. Indeed, there are striking examples of Christian groups around the world today which are clearly connecting with their modern-day societies, successfully retaining their young people, and readily recruiting new members. However, many other Christian denominations and congregations (in addition to the Church of Christ) are experiencing a downward slope, for much the same reasons. Also, it is not just religious groups that are shrinking, many non-profit clubs and other volunteer organizations are also in decline.

Although indirect societal mechanisms are affecting all sorts of volunteer, nonprofit groups across-the-board, I contend that practical solutions based on Jesus' teachings and Jesus' methods would benefit them as well the Church of Christ. Thus they may also find this constructive criticism useful, although it does specifically addressed my own inherited religious group, the Church of Christ.

Furthermore, my advice is directed specifically to the so-called "mainline" Church of Christ congregations. Sadly, from my experience with them, the so-called Church of Christ "splinter-groups" have so crippled themselves with severely-restrictive traditions that I see no hope for their remaining few, tiny, remnant-congregations.

I ask a stark question of the leadership of mainline Church of Christ congregations: *"What do you want?"* If it's to maintain the traditions of shrinking congregations until both you and they die-out, then just continue on same course you are on now. If it's to do effective personal and local evangelism (as every preacher I've ever heard in my life claim is our collective and individual #1 duty), your present methods are failing. (Note that although helping anyone anywhere to move closer to God is laudable, setting aside a small amount of money to send overseas to maintain a tiny congregation half a world away that's dependent upon your continued support is by definition *not* effective personal or local evangelism.) If it is to connect with the people around us in our present-day society as we together struggle to follow the radical teachings of Jesus in joyful pursuit of greater Godliness---then you've got the right idea, if not the right methods.

I respectfully offer practical solutions that might help reverse the slide which threatens to permanently close the doors of most of these congregations. The "take-home message" to my specific suggestions listed below (for accomplishing the latter *AIM* noted in the paragraph above) is as simple as it is offensive and radical: *STOP PUTTING TRADITION ABOVE JESUS*! Yes, I know you say that your traditional beliefs and practices are exactly what Jesus wants you to do, but any intelligent person taking an unbiased look at the Gospels would doubt your claim.

Although many people do adopt and continue their involvement with formal religion for the explicit purpose of being part of an established religious Tradition (with its safely-enshrined beliefs, doctrines, rituals, and ceremonies), refusal to even consider anything deeper than the "status-quo" is a recipe for stagnation and decline. Whether you like it or not, the world moves on, societal priorities change, and the valid perceived needs of people shift.

Yes, what actually does continue to work for achieving one's objectives is certainly worth maintaining. But honoring the status quo as one's #1 objective in religion---regardless of its ability in the prevailing circumstance to achieve desired objectives---is *not* what Jesus taught! In fact, JESUS WAS A DISRUPTER OF THE STATUS QUO!

Furthermore, JESUS DID NOT COME TO MAKE OUR LIFE SIMPLE, EASY, AND SAFE! Our natural inclination as humans is to take the extremely-challenging teachings and actions of Jesus and turn them into comfortable platitudes, set rituals, and predictable procedures---in other words, have Jesus make us into slightly-improved Jewish people of his time. However, the result of "taming" the *dangerous* Jesus is often boredom, lack of achievement, and a failure to inspire other people.

Fully embracing the *radical* Jesus is dangerous, complicated, and difficult. However, putting the *real* Jesus #1 (see my book on the subject: "The Real Jesus") by placing follow him even higher than our most-cherished, inherited traditions---can be tremendously exciting and productive!

Although I'm deliberately not making this treatise a "proof-text" sermon (in order to not have involved, detailed, proof-text debating obscure the overall "take-home messages") I invite you to look again at the clear scriptures from the New Testament stating that all Jesus' disciples should: 1) "put on" Jesus, 2) "have the mind" of Jesus, 3) follow in his footsteps, and 4) do as He did. In other words, Jesus' disciples are authoritatively ordered to look like him, think like him, and replicate his actions.

These noble goals, however---though occasionally acknowledged in sermons---are often constrained, restricted, chopped-to-pieces, and dissipated by our love of comfortably-safe tradition. Or, we discount Jesus' examples for us by saying: "But that's Jesus, the Son of God! We're not Jesus and we can't do what He did!" But can we not *try* to get *as close* to his Example as is possible for us mere humans in our present-day society? Can we not hold Jesus up as our benchmark?

Also, Jesus is often looked at as merely the initiator of his subsequent church doctrines which apparently "trumps" his previous teachings and examples! Yet was not the "New Testament Church" supposedly striving to be like Jesus, and in many cases falling far short? Don't fall back on making excuses! If we as Christians stop following Jesus as our #1 objective---greater even than honoring our traditional beliefs and practices---then we lose the enthusiasm and nimbleness necessary to successfully connect with our modern-day society.

Typically, church leadership as articulated in public sermons blames two things for the obvious steady decline of their congregations: 1) bad membership in the congregation, or 2) bad people in the world. Yes, this harsh criticism is often veiled by railing against science, the entertainment industry, or Satan. But the clear "bottom-line" fault is laid on people (our youth, us sitting in the pews, or people outside our congregation) for "giving in" to supposedly ungodly influences.

Let me just set the record straight. Your membership is not composed of bad people who fail to love God enough! Likewise, the people in our society are no worse or more distracted by work/pleasure than they were in Jesus' time! Stop making excuses! If you, the church leadership, must blame someone, blame yourselves! Stop loving your traditions more than Jesus! Stop seeking that which is comfortable: simple, easy, and safe! Put Jesus first and foremost above all else even if it is complicated, hard, and a bit dangerous!

In the following chapters I list 50 practical suggestions for reversing the decline, based upon what we know of Jesus' actions and teachings in the Gospels. These integrated, comprehensive recommendations are grouped under seven overall chapter headings: *"The Worship Service," "Group Meetings," "Doctrine," "Evangelism," "Church Management," "Church Leadership,"* and *"Crisis Management."* Included under each of the 50 general recommendations are specific, practical "Possible Action Items."

Adopting these achievable steps would revolutionize most mainline Church of Christ congregations: restoring the dynamism, excitement, and joy of being a disciple of Jesus Christ! Failure to do so will result in more of the same: an increasingly-large disconnect with one's present-day society, little or no effective personal or local evangelism, established members quietly slipping out the back door, and our precious children---once they get out on their own---quitting or going elsewhere.

In summary, what is the solution? Tradition has its place. Tradition is important and useful. But tradition should not be put above Jesus. Jesus should come first. Instead of following tradition, we should follow Jesus.

All my life the preachers of the mainline Church of Christ have publicly claimed that we are *not* a denomination. When people ask us what we are religiously, these preachers say we're *not* to say that we are "Church of Christers" but say that we are Christians! Now is the time to put this claim into action!

From what people see of us it seems obvious to them that despite our rhetoric we actually identify ourselves by our handed-down traditional beliefs and practices, just as do all the other Christian denominations. *It is time that we identified ourselves in truth as people who think, talk, and act like Jesus!*

-----------------------------------------------------------------

# 50 Specific Suggestions:

## Chapter One:

## THE WORSHIP SERVICE

1) **Stop being proud of being boring** --- JESUS WAS NOT BORING!

Attempting to be the "intellectuals" of the Christian denominational world, most mainline Church of Christ congregations discourage and reject overt signs of emotion during their services. Thus the more *un*emotional the service or Bible Study the better! This is the excuse of many a boring preacher, boring Bible class "teacher," and defensive Elder---that we are appropriately being intellectual rather than emotional. No. You are not being "intellectual," you are being boring.

If your services, classes, and interactions with people in the community are boring, this will *not* inspire your people, *not* attract visitors, and *not* convince your youth to stay once they've matured. So just *how* do you appropriately "not be boring"? Attempting to be Intellectuals, many preachers and Bible teachers deliver sermons and classes focused on having the "right" doctrines. Although doctrine is certainly important---both as self-definition characteristics and enabling church framework---most people are not interested in them beyond acquiring an initial understanding and acceptance.

Also, doctrine can easily be incorporated into sermons and classes focused primarily on other topics, such as: 1) Jesus, 2) problems facing people in our present society, and 3) how to implement the radical principles of Jesus taking advantage of opportunities for personal spiritual growth! The three topics I just mentioned are *interesting* if well-presented: Jesus, problems, and opportunities!

Also, boring people with an over-emphasis on doctrine will *not* inspire your young people, edify your members, or intrigue your visitors! Yes, you are successfully "defending the Truth"---but what does it matter if your people are bored and don't come back? A number of the following 49 points will address additional specifics of how to (appropriately) not be boring.

But the answer to this sad, un-Christ-like condition is certainly *NOT* to defensively say: "Well, you *should* be excited and amazed by what I/we say and do!" If it's boring, it's boring.

Furthermore, saying that people should somehow be filled with Joy yet have no outward sign thereof is illogical. In most mainline Church of Christ congregations the clapping or raising of hands during singing, speaking an audible "Amen!" or "Preach on, Preacher!" during a sermon, or a happy "yelp"---even though done to collectively energize and inspire each other---will get a person "shushed" if not kicked out!

Following are some general ways to make things (appropriately) *INTERESTING!* These possible Action Items will be addressed in more detail in following points.

**Possible Action Items:**
- *Sing visibly joyfully.*
- Preachers start with *a real problem or opportunity* of your members.
- *Project* the sermon and words to songs up on a large screen at the front of the congregation.
- Have a *variety of excellent, knowledgeable presenters* on desired, assigned topics.
- Bible class teachers focus on *asking important, intriguing discussion questions*, then facilitating spirited targeted discussion...rather than pontificating.

- Have well-integrated, deliberately-*impactful services and classes.*
- *Combine theory with application* in equal proportions.
- Allow and even *encourage an occasional "Amen, Brother!"* during sermons.

2) **Instead of beating people up, *build* them up** --- JESUS CHOSE TO BUILD GOOD-HEARTED PEOPLE UP RATHER THAN JUST CONDEMN THEM FOR THEIR EVER-PRESENT FAULTS!

Unfortunately, it's far easier to beat up on people than to *build* them up. Thus, a favorite topic of many preachers is defaulting to the "easy" sermon: on how poorly the members of their congregations are supposedly doing at "evangelizing" and other Christian activities.

A second favorite topic is how evil the people of the world are at not wanting to flock into the open doors of the church building. Yes, this is so pervasive among preachers that many Christians don't feel like they've "done church" unless they've been suitably chastised!

Here are some common-sense ways that preachers, Bible teachers, and church leaders can work to *BUILD UP* their people:

**Possible Action Items:**
- *Publicly acknowledge* when people do well in serving God and the congregation.
- *Say "thank you"* when people do good things: specifically, timely, and sincerely.
- *Make it easy to do good things* (providing appropriate support, structure, and mandate).
- *Provide opportunity* for people to offer their talents to well-functioning programs.

..............................................................

3) **Change preaching and teaching of the Bible from doctrine-focused to problem-focused** --- JESUS CONNECTED DIRECTLY WITH HIS SOCIETY'S WORST COLLECTIVE AND INDIVIDUAL PROBLEMS!

The biggest concern of Jesus' audiences was the occupation and subjugation of their land under the heavy hand of the Roman Empire. Jesus used this over-riding, critical concern to preach the Kingdom of God---but not as an earthly kingdom, rather as a spiritual reality.

Much of Jesus' preaching was an education on converting one's heart from a den of selfishness into a place where God would dwell as King, a message the people cared little about. But this transcendental teaching was well-received when "piggy-backed" upon the immediate, pressing concern of the people to have their own kingdom!

Likewise, the tradition of being the "intellectuals" of Christianity harps on doctrine. Most of Church of Christ sermons and classes focus on the "right" doctrine: i.e. what's the right position on some issue. People are not interested in doctrine! And yet the mainline Church of Christ sermons and Bible classes are mostly doctrine.

Not only is connecting the "proper" scriptures together with the "correct" inferences of little interest to anyone (*especially when repeated over and over to people who already know and agree on those doctrines*), it is boring (see point #1).

If sermons and Bible classes do as Jesus did---starting with a clear pressing problem that people are suffering from---*THE SAME SCRIPTURES CAN THEN BE PRESENTED IN A FRAMEWORK PEOPLE WILL ACCEPT WITH STRONG INTEREST!*

Another way of saying this is that Church of Christ sermons and classes need to be "relevant" to their audience. Of course, this is much more difficult, complicated, and even dangerous than just taking a random reading from the Bible and pontificating upon its inherent doctrines. However, directly connecting to the immediate life problems and opportunities of your members, visitors, and youth can keep their interest while providing meaningful impact.

**Possible Action Items:**
- *Ask your people* in appropriate ways and forums to identify the main problems they face.
- *Prioritize* those real problems/opportunities and organize them in a logical sequence.
- *Plan a whole year* of relevant, meaningful problems/opportunities to address in your congregation.
- *Organize* services and classes around Bible solutions for study; plus active application of Biblical solutions to pressing problems.

. . . . . . . . . . . . . . . . . . . . . . . . . . . . . . . . . . . . . . . . . . . . . . . . . . . . .

**4) Place your focus on doing the Good (and HOW to do it) rather than just condemning sin** --- JESUS' AIM WAS TO HELP MANKIND MOVE CLOSER TO GOD VIA BUILDING ON THE POSITIVES OF PEOPLE!

Recently, even the head of the largest Christian group, the Catholic Church, made a stir by changing their emphasis from cutting out the negatives to expanding the positives. This did not mean a change in their beliefs or doctrines. However, it did mean a change in what members, visitors, and youth would experience. Instead of trying to motivate people through fear and guilt, it meant motivating by love and gratitude. The idea is that by growing and expanding the positives, the negatives can be crowded out!

Furthermore, by focusing not just on the positives but HOW to do the positives---specific techniques, methods, and tools---people acquire useful information in actually making their lives more Godly.

Again, this moves sermons, Bible lessons, and agendas from almost useless vague generalities to actual productivity. But this is hard to do! It is far easier to rail against some dysfunctional, evil system than to find ways that work to pull it from the abyss and reform it. This is why my book here isn't just pointing out faults, but offering specific, practical Action Items for real improvements!

A typical example in Church of Christ congregations is to condemn sexual practices that deviate from the norm while offering little or nothing to support and enhance healthy marriages! To help foundering marriages means acquiring and successfully applying a great deal of expert knowledge on human relations, psychology, and conflict resolution. To condemn sexual malpractice is a simple matter of railing against the "lax" practices of modern-day society.

Often, it's not even a Bible-based reasonable study of positives and negatives, but merely rote doctrinal declarations. As such, the proclamation to behave sexually in a Godly manner falls on deaf ears. However, a spirited defense of the best practices combined with helpful specifics can turn a boring lecture or class into an interesting and helpful presentation/discussion that people are actually glad to have attended and participated in.

**Possible Action Items:**
- In sermons instead of stopping at "What?" *continue on to "Why?"* (not just "God says to!"---but actual justification as to its value to people) *and especially "HOW?"* to really do it!
- Give real-life, *contemporary EXAMPLES* of people struggling with the "Why?" and "HOW?"
- *Bring in experts* in that particular subject to give talks and classes on specifics.
- In classes, after establishing the "What?" spend most of the time *prompting the participants to productive discussion* by asking them "Why?" and "HOW?"

.............................................................

**5) Change "preaching" and "lecturing" into "*value-added learning*"** --- JESUS TAUGHT PEOPLE SO THAT THEY WERE INTRIGUED TO TEACH THEMSELVES!

Let me ask you a serious question: "What good does it do to spend your valuable time preparing a sermon or lesson on something that the audience already knows and believes?" If the people are reasonably intelligent, not only will they resent being preached at or lectured on things they already know and accept, but they'll also be bored stiff!

During your next church service or Bible class, look closely at the faces of the people in front of or around you (of course not in a way they'd see and be offended at). If they have blank, sad, or distant expressions then they are not getting anything out of the proceedings! Sadly, many of the sermons and classes of mainline Church of Christ congregations when judged from the expressions of the people present seem a waste of valuable time, both in the preparation and the hearing! However, if you truly give the people something that *THEY* will agree was of value, then they'll be interested enough to *want* to come back---not just to reluctantly return out of a sense of painful duty.

It's a cliché to speak of a preacher at the end of his sermon fervently encouraging people to come forward to be baptized when he knows full well that everyone there has already done such! Unfortunately, I've witnessed this too often. In fact, I witnessed it happening just a week ago! The fervent, futile admonishment was merely a traditional, doctrinal habit being expressed rather than giving those particular people something of real value helping them to move closer to God!

Furthermore, it's not just a case of "here's the answer" lecturing! The best preaching, as exemplified by Jesus, tantalizes people with *new* information while leaving key question *un*-answered! In this way, JESUS CAUSED THE PEOPLE TO GO AWAY, DISCUSS AMONGST THEMSELVES, PUZZLE

IN THEIR OWN BRAINS, AND THEN COME UP WITH "THE" ANSWERS THEMSELVES! Jesus knew full well that the best way to get a compelling Answer to "stick" was to help the people to discover it on their own!

Can this be done by us mere-human preachers and teachers today? The answer is "yes"---though it requires quite a bit more thought, preparation, and depth than is typically put into traditional sermons and classes. Again, I ask: "What do you want?" Do you want people going away from your sermons or lectures with the memory that something was said about something in the Bible---can't quite remember what---or with a helpful new insight on how to truly move closer to God?

**Possible Action Items:**
- Instead of merely presenting in a sermon or lecture the traditional understanding on some Bible passage, *consider its practical APPLICATION* to modern-day problems or opportunities of the people in your audience.
- Consider the *LEVEL OF KNOWLEDGE* of your audience---not just when averaged, but *how many at each level* are present!
- *Weight the depth of knowledge presented* according to the needs of the people in your audience (such as not having to dwell on "milk" for a spiritually-mature audience).
- Speak or teach to present in every sermon or class *at least one thing of value that's not already known* by your audience or subgroups therein.
- Instead of being "the Authority" handing down ready-made answers, strive to *INTRIGUE your audience with examples and questions* for which there is no "right or wrong" answer!

. . . . . . . . . . . . . . . . . . . . . . . . . . . . . . . . . . . . . . . . . . . . . . . . . . . . . . .

6) **Sing visibly joyfully and well** --- JESUS' BIRTH WAS HERALDED BY A CHORUS OF ANGELS!

One of the most moving and powerful experience of corporate (group) Christian gatherings is the singing...when it is done well! Unfortunately, mainline Church of Christ traditions often produce a stunted, strained, and lackluster "corporate" singing experience. Why?

Well, first of all there is a proscription (ban) against any musical instruments used with singing, which borders on paranoia! Even a "tuning pipe" for a song leader to use in order to start a song at the correct note is frowned upon. Not using a ready means to start at the proper note results in making it extra-difficult to sing already-difficult songs when they are too often pitched too high or too low. Whereas other Christian groups have no problem using all sorts of beautiful-sounding instruments to supplement and complement the human voice, mainline Church of Christ congregations can't.

Yet according to the Bible, man-made musical instruments were fine to help praise God with in Jewish worship (as clearly seen in the Old Testament) and at the end of time in heaven (as depicted in the book of Revelation). However, according to Church of Christ traditional doctrine, God in the Christian time-period now *hates* it---and those who use it are "worshipping in error"! This is puzzling as there is no such prohibition in the pages of the New Testament.

Somehow it was fine with God in the Old Testament times, ok with God to use in heaven after the judgment day (whether that's symbolic language or not), but in between God hates it---though He somehow forget to mention it in the New Testament!

To an unbiased reader of the Bible, a prohibition against using musical instruments in Christian worship is clearly a doctrine that's been added to the New Testament. Preachers of the Church of Christ, though, are non-the-less adamant on this prohibition. Actually, it is one of the defining characteristics of Church of Christ doctrine, rooted in historical precedence.

The Church of Christ denomination began in the 19th century as an off-shoot of the Christian Church, splitting from them over the doctrinal question of using instruments in church singing. Thus---even though most Church of Christ members aren't even aware of the historical importance of the issue---it is in their handed-down religious "DNA" as one of their most important traditional doctrines. (This fact is rarely mentioned by preachers or Bible teachers because it would confirm that the Church of Christ is merely another Christian denomination among many others, rather than being the "true" church started way back in the first century.)

This unfortunate traditional doctrine contributes to a poor worship or class experience that "turns-off" visitors, bores young people, and even kills the joy of the regular membership (though they are largely unaware of its negative impact).

Compounding this drag on the potentially-powerful impact of corporate church singing is the traditional use of complex "four-part-harmony" song books. These are difficult songs with little repetition of words except in the chorus (where the words are also often a complex sequence). In addition, anything other than singing by the entire group is also banned, meaning that a beautiful solo or choral group cannot sing the verses even though everyone might be invited to join in on the repeating chorus.

In smaller congregations (which the mainline Church of Christ is mostly composed of) it is even not unusual for there to be little or no harmony! Whereas most people might be able to follow-along the melody, to sing the alto, tenor, and base parts requires particular rare training and talents. Having little or no good harmony further "deadens" the singing service. Even singing only the melody of songs is a talent that not everyone possesses. And certainly to sing well is a rare talent.

Without a trained chorus of talented singers to fall back on, all members are stuck struggling to keep up with non-repeating verse-wordage and complicated musical notes, their noses buried in their complex song books, struggling with hard melodies and parts---their expressions of difficult, pained work often at marked odds with the words of exultation and praise coming from their very own lips.

One could argue how ridiculous this is from a Bible standpoint since the complicated four-part harmony songs were written long after the New Testament was penned. However, having become a part of tradition in years past, their use has been "sanctified" almost as much as if they were actually written into the Bible! In fact, these particular complex tunes are so sanctified that singing any newer songs (most of the accepted songs in the commonly-used Church of Christ song books were written one or two hundred years ago) is either suspect or out-right forbidden.

Other Christian groups, however, are free to use powerful instrumental supplementation, expert song leaders, trained choral groups, solo presentations, simpler songs with repeating words, and newer songs that speak to the present generation---to easily produce powerful, impactful, group-praise/edification song sessions! Of course there's nothing inherently "wrong" with a cappella singing, particularly if it's done well. Many mainline Church of Christ congregations, unfortunately, do not even do their a cappella singing well. Visitors, youth, and even long-term members go away unimpressed, "turned-off" by the visibly-*joyless* singing!

If Church of Christ congregations cannot bring themselves to repudiate their historical roots on this issue (which is quite understandable since it's one of their main self-identification doctrines), then they could go a long ways toward improving their singing by adopting some of the other easy techniques that I've listed below.  As the Bible says, singing should be done "with the spirit and with the understanding." Knowledge alone or Emotion alone fails.

Church of Christ congregations have plenty of understanding in their singing, but little or no obvious joy.  Help make your corporate assembly be more attractive with visibly-joyful singing rather than appearing as an obviously-tedious, discouraging chore!

**Possible Action Items:**
- Use modern technology to *project the words* of the songs onto a large screen in front of the audience (so people can look at the song leader, look at each other, and see their expressions reflected in the faces of others).
- Incorporate occasional "performances" by *expert singers and singing groups* into the services, to which the audience respectfully listens (or might join in on during repetitive choruses).
- Incorporate some *"praise"-type simpler songs* along with the complex four-part harmony songs into the services (that can be remembered easily, freeing a person from studying a text).
- Look for an occasional *totally-new (to your people) song of particular impact* to include in your service (practiced in advance by sufficient numbers).
- Have *"song practice" sessions* with interested people in your congregation (whether in a formal choral group of not) to actually work on "new" songs in your songbook not previously sung by your congregation, for use in services once a "critical mass" of singers knows it (approximately a third of the songs in the official, large songbooks aren't sung at all in any particular congregation).

- Encourage appropriately-talented people in your congregation (particularly young people) to *write your own songs*, the best of which are honored by being sung in the services!
- *STOP SINGING A RANDOM SELECTION OF UNRELATED SONGS!* Have an impactful logical sequence of closely-related songs on a Theme for the service, in which each successive song builds upon the others (such as directly supporting the topic of the sermon or class)!

..................................................

7) **Institute well-organized, impactful services rather than rote rituals** --- JESUS MADE A POWERFUL IMPACT WHENEVER HE HELD AN EVENT!

The concept of "boring" or "wasting time" did not apply to the events that Jesus initiated. This is because he and his close disciples carefully organized and orchestrated his events to have a maximal desired impact! Yes, this is complicated, difficult, and even somewhat dangerous---to have deliberate programs rather than repetitive rituals. But it is far better to have people leave your present-day Christian events saying "That was really interesting and helpful! I'm sure glad we went there today!" rather than to have them sigh and say: "Well, we did it again..."!!

Sadly, attendance to Church of Christ services and classes is often compelled by: "A verse in the Bible says to not forsake the assembly of yourself together" or "You're supposed to obey what your leaders decide is best for you" or "If you fall away you're going to hell"... in other words, out of a sense of duty and fear rather than joyful anticipation!

Once again, *LOOK AT THE FACES OF THE PEOPLE IN YOUR SERVICE OR CLASS*! Do they look like they're struggling just to stay awake? Or are they smiling, engaged, and excited? Don't take my word for what's actually going on in your assemblies. Look for yourself! Is the purpose of your gatherings to "do it again" or to "help people happily move closer to God"?

I myself am infamous for giving interesting talks that truly engage all the people present, including the youth! I do so with an engaging, useful topic combined with excellent visuals and a tight presentation! And yet I am rarely allowed to do this, as the leadership at the number of congregations I've attended over the years often deliberately excludes me from doing so! Why? Because it is "controversial" to do anything beyond mouthing mere traditional doctrines!

Is it any wonder that Jesus was often banned from preaching in the Temple and Synagogues! Not only did he bring up "dangerous" topics, but JESUS DEMONSTRATED BY HIS OWN ACTIONS THAT IT WAS INDEED POSSIBLE TO GIVE RELIGIOUS PRESENTATIONS THAT WERE TRULY INTERESTING, EXCITING, USEFUL, AND MOTIVATING TO HIS AUDIENCE!

You can claim your speeches are "golden"---but an audience filled with struggling-to-stay-awake people puts the lie to your boast. Yes, you are correct that the purpose of church is not to entertain people. But an *un*interesting, *un*edifying, *un*inspiring, *un*helpful, and *dis*organized, "mish-mash" service or class is a waste of time!

It is common practice in Church of Christ congregations to have a sermon on one topic (if the audience is lucky; likely it is a mixture of several loosely-related topics that confuses and bores people, relinquishing any meaningful impact in the zeal to "teach the Bible"), plus songs unrelated to the topic or to each other, plus prayers poorly articulated on a variety of random topics, plus a communion-introduction on yet some other aspect of the Bible.

*EVEN IF THE PIECES OF A SERVICE OR CLASS INDIVIDUALLY ARE COMPELLING, HAVING A MISH-MASH OF DIFFERENT TOPICS LEAVES THE AUDIENCE DAZED AND CONFUSED!*

*It is not difficult to have a tightly-focused sermon, songs on that topic, prayers slanted in that direction, and a communion talk that echoes the overall theme!* Other Christian groups are able to do this! Doing anything less will dilute the impact of the service, appear amateurish, and *de*motivate visitors, youth, and even members from returning.

**Possible Action Items:**
- *Have a Theme*, such as the preacher's sermon topic.
- *Project the Theme* title up at the beginning of the service on a large screen in front of the congregation and keep it there.
- Get the people together who will participate in leading the service sometime before the service to *plan out their activities to support the theme.*
- *Select songs on the theme*, that fit together in a logical sequence. Again, STOP SINGING A RANDOM MISH-MASH OF UNRELATED SONGS!
- If the communion is offered, have the *introductory remarks reflect the theme.*
- Have those wording *prayers consider the theme* in their statements.
- Make sure a *closing prayer focuses on summing up* Action Items related to the theme of the service, asking God to help us to actually implement them!

------------------------------------------------

### Chapter Two:

## GROUP MEETINGS

8) **Discover your Objectives and optimize your procedures for best-achieving them** --- EVERYTHING JESUS DID HAD A CLEAR PURPOSE!

Yes, it's ok to have your Objective for your services and classes, if you wish, to be "honor tradition." Just be upfront about it (such as putting on your sign out front of the building: *"Traditional Services and Classes"*) while *not* expecting that you'll be able to retain your young people, intrigue visitors, or keep your existing membership.

A good example of Tradition trumping Purpose is the *second* worship service that most mainline Church of Christ congregations insist on having each Sunday. This is a repeat of the exact same things done in the a.m. service. Why? Was there something wrong done in the morning service that needs to be corrected by going back for an evening duplicate service?

What, then, was the original purpose of having a second, duplicate worship service on Sunday? I've heard that the Sunday evening service came into being in rural settings where farmers and ranchers could not set aside their morning chores (such as milking the cows) and therefore could not attend on Sunday mornings. I've also heard that when cars became common with their accompanying Sunday drives out of town that the second, duplicate service allowed them a convenient time to stop by in the evening to go to church. Another story about the origin of the practice was that when businesses began staying open on Sundays, a second evening worship allowed those required to work during the day to attend after their work was finished.

In whatever way the second duplicate service began, though, it soon became a tradition promoted with the same fervor as any other doctrine.  What demonstrates this most vividly is when some congregations stick the second worship service after a lunch-break.  It's an obvious attempt to not have people have to go home then come back.  But if it's during the day hours, any attempt to justify it other than tradition is made mute!  So the true reason it exists today is certainly tradition, nothing more!

Indeed, the "good" members are those that attended the second evening service---not just because they missed the morning service, but out of their "enthusiasm" to hear yet another sermon!  Really?  Thus the second service is a "test" for being a "good" member: i.e. whether or not you will attend church *TWICE* on Sunday!  Note that this is certainly *not* a practice mandated in the scriptures!  The "best" members, however, became those that not only attended twice on Sundays but also at the "midweek Bible study"---a practice that's also not found in the scriptures.

Is there anything inherently wrong with corporate gatherings of Christians occurring several times a week?  Certainly not!  In fact, according to the book of Acts, when the Christian church began the people met *daily* "from house to house."  If Church of Christ congregations wanted to blindly follow Bible precedence, they'd have church gatherings every day!

I'm sure the answer would be: "That's not practical!"  But if "church attendance" is what determines one's "value" as a Christian in God's sight, why not do as many Catholic congregations have done for years, offering a "morning-mass" each day?  Or why not have duplicate services (not just because of the legitimate reason that there may be too many people to attend all at one meeting-time inside the building) *ten* times each Sunday?

At an hour each, you could indeed fairly easily conduct ten duplicate worship services on each and every Sunday!  Instead of two sermons, the members could hear ten sermons!

But most of us see how ridiculous and unenforceable such a requirement would be. Thus "pushing the equation to its limits" (as is routinely done in higher mathematics) helps us understand a practice's validity and shortcomings! It is typical at an evening Sunday service of the Church of Christ to have few or no people who missed that morning, thus obviating any functional purpose!

But if Christianity is more than just quantity, why not adopt a "value-added" purpose to that extra meeting to which incredibly-dedicated members attend out of a sense of unspecified duty (honoring tradition whether or not it makes any sense)? Sure, those that missed the morning service can still be taken to the side afterwards or at the first of the meeting to be given the (weekly-required, though this weekly requirement isn't in the New Testament) communion, while *still* proceeding with a different, "value-added" protocol!

It's been said (I learned this from a minister of mine some years in the past, Steve Keller) that people have three main inward religiously-expressed needs: 1) to Worship; 2) to Fellowship; and 3) be of Service. This makes a lot of sense. In our society where it's ASKING A LOT OF PEOPLE TO COME TO TWO DIFFERENT TIME-PERIODS FOR CHURCH THINGS PER WEEK the mainline Church of Christ congregations ask for <u>FOUR</u> TIME-PERIODS (Sunday morning Bible class, Sunday morning worship, Sunday evening worship, and midweek Bible class). Then, after that's all done, we're told, in essence, "*NOW* go out and do good things for the congregation!"

There's no time left---especially to do things where we need to pool our talents together! *Tradition has trumped and largely destroyed the key purposes of meaningful Fellowship and productive Service!* Since "worship" has already been well-accomplished Sunday morning, why not use Sunday evening or midweek gatherings to combine the incredibly-talented passions of the membership for the overt purposes of Fellowship or Service?

Yes, Bible-study when done in comfortable, small-group, home-settings can certainly also provide powerful Fellowship. In addition, Service can indeed incorporate targeted Bible-study as well, while also furthering Fellowship! The critical point is to *CLEARLY KNOW WHAT YOU ARE TRYING TO ACHIEVE* (versus just proceeding on "autopilot" honoring Tradition as the unspoken objective); and then *optimize* the procedure to best-achieve the clearly-stated Purpose!

You can bore your young people, visitors, and members with ritualistic repetitions---or *invigorate* them by meeting their valid spiritual needs! None of these things are mandated to be done in some exact way in the scriptures.

The New Testament simply *does not say* how to "do church." A sprinkling of a few isolated verses stitched together with traditional assumptions as a "pattern" is what's used to justify the procedures of Church of Christ gatherings. Yet not only the details but the biggest things in modern-day church services (such as church buildings, paid local ministers, or worship services themselves) aren't even mentioned in the scriptures! It's your choice as to whether or not your group meetings are organized in ways best suited to meeting a defined Purpose other than just "let's do it again."

For instance, is your Worship service's objective to: "Celebrate and enthuse people for Jesus and God"? Is your Bible class purpose to: "Help people see how Jesus' teachings can help them be better, more-successful people"? Is a midweek small group's purpose to: "Provide a friendly, non-threatening forum to bring people to Jesus"? Is the youth program's purpose to: "Enthuse our young-people for following Jesus?" Is an outreach work group's purpose to: "Find and recruit local people to our congregation?" Is the Sunday sermon's purpose to: "Provide intriguing Bible information for Sunday evening or midweek small-group home studies to meaningfully discuss?" Is a small group midweek program to: "Promote meaningful discussion of the sermon topics?" or to "Provide friendly spiritual fellowship to which we can readily invite friends and family?"

These Objectives, of course, are just examples. The point is to *know what you are trying to do, determine if that is actually happening, and adjust your methods to better succeed if you are failing*!

**Possible Action Items:**
- *Decide on Objectives* of what you're trying to achieve---for all your various services and group meetings.
- *Evaluate by real data* (attendance numbers, solicited feedback from attendees, and real achievements) if you are meeting the Objectives.
- *Consider adjusting* your Methods to better-meet your Objectives.
- *Test your adjustments* by real data to see if they improve your results.
- *Repeat* the above steps on into the future.

..............................................................

9) **Provide regular "church time" to actually *DO* together (rather than just talk about), the teachings of Jesus** --- JESUS COMBINED SERVICE WITH TEACHING!

As I've discussed above, at most Church of Christ congregations the "best" members are expected to attend *four* church-gatherings per week, namely: 1) Sunday morning Bible classes, 2) Sunday morning worship service, 3) Sunday evening worship service, and 4) midweek Bible studies. A few progressive congregations have incorporated small-group home Bible studies in place of either the Sunday evening or midweek gatherings at the church building.

However, what has all this heroic church attendance per week accomplished? Once again, the Tradition being honored is to be the "intellectuals" of the Christian world---going over and over the same scriptures!

Of course for any new members or children, an initial close examination of the key parts of the Bible is quite valuable! After a short period of time, though, most members quickly understand the main "take-home messages" of the Bible, accept the doctrines on how verses should best be fitted-together, and are well-aware of the main things about Jesus.

These "first-principles" are what is referred to in the Bible as "milk." Milk is quite valuable for spiritual babes in Christ to "drink" and from which to grow. But quickly the spiritual babies mature into spiritual adults who then should (according to the New Testament) quickly move on from milk to the meat! Church of Christ preachers, teachers, and leaders seem not to have gotten this message. They are largely fixated on the milk of the Bible.

Indeed, the milk is even presented as if the adult spiritual members were still physical children---making it into *skim-milk!* "Mickey-Mouse" type grade-school "Bible-study" booklets and forms demean the intelligence of the audience!

So what, then, is this "meat" which matured spiritual Christians should put into their minds and life? Some think it is complicated doctrines and difficult topics. No. From the example of Jesus, plus other key New Testament passages, the "meat" is quite simply the *APPLICATION* of the teachings of Jesus!

Church of Christ tradition is to spend virtually all of the "church" time to do "Bible study" (mostly sermons and lectures) of one sort or another. The application thereof is then assumed to be an individual responsibility, done outside of the formal church study periods. Unfortunately, in our complex world where we are faced with difficult problems and opportunities, Christians need to work together in a highly organized and synergistic manner to make real progress. In Church of Christ congregations little or no time is allowed for Christians to actually work together in a regular, sustained, and effective manner.

I remember as a youth being made ashamed by the constant chiding of the Preacher that I could alone somehow bring others to services. So I fearfully tried to invite a friend of mine to come to church services! It turned out that he was already a member of another Christian group well-known for their work applying Jesus' teachings to help the downtrodden and disadvantaged. He concluded his brief reply to my invitation by stating with obvious sincerity and enthusiasm: "I am so *proud* of my church!" I, in turn, had no reply to give back. I knew that at the church building we had a clothes room filled with old clothes imbedded in moth balls...that no one ever wanted. I knew that we had a pantry from which we'd grudgingly give a few cans of food to beggars if they came to the building. But nothing we did in any way compared to what his group was doing in actually living out the teachings of Jesus. In fact, *I had never heard any Church of Christ member ever say anything similar about their congregation!*

Furthermore, my first mental response was what I'd been programmed from a child to think was #1 above all else: *doctrine*! The arguments popped into my brain about how we should not being proud of things...about the church not being ours but being Jesus'...which immediately were deflated by the realization that quibbling over the wording of his statement next to the reality of what that other group was actually accomplishing on a daily basis would be stupid. So my mouth literally hung open with no words coming out.

My friend had innocently put both me and "my" church literally in our place: empty words... Tradition, though, *is* very powerful. Traditional doctrines---even when clearly not in the Bible---often becomes sanctified as if it were in the Bible.

I recall so vividly when I ran a very productive small group on Sunday evenings. During a so-called "liberal" phase of that congregation, work groups were initiated on Sunday evenings. The particular work group I headed up was in pooling the talents of several of us members to facilitated Singles meetings, planning and running periodic within-or-across-congregational gatherings for single Christians, and setting up computer systems for the church. It was very productive and enjoyable.

However, after a couple years, things changed. The so-called liberal leaders departed and the conservatives came back to power. One of the first things they did was to make a public announcement on Sunday morning that even though doing things for Christ was a good idea, those efforts should be done at some time other than Sunday evenings---when they wanted all the people gathered together in the auditorium!

Being a cooperative, "submissive" member I did as ordered, shutting down the internet websites we'd been building, terminating the talents-assessment system we'd been putting into place, taking my computer gear home (since the leadership hadn't supported us financially I'd brought my own equipment in), and informed the others that our years-long Singles activities were finished. Our group did not have unlimited time that they could just "find another time" to work together to implement the teachings of Jesus!

The Leadership got what they wanted: a few more passive members sitting like bumps on logs on a pew being lectured-at on things they already knew perfectly well. Tradition (in the form of a group duplicate worship service neither found nor mandated in the Bible) trumped Principle. They won! But they lost far more than they gained... All the good works we'd together been successfully doing for the congregation stopped.

By the way, it was only a few months more before the congregation shrank to almost closing its doors, the leadership that killed the "liberal" activities having resigned or quit the congregation entirely. It took a number of years to partially-recover from that retrenchment.

**Possible Action Items:**
- Take away one or more of the duplicate services and replace it or them with *active work groups*---where like-talented and interested people spend that time planning and implementing together effective programs "*doing* the Truth" rather than just talking about it.
- And/or *add a strong and regular APPLICATION component* into existing Bible class or small-group studies.
- For instance, still gather on Sunday evening if that's the habit of your congregation---but after a short 15-minute devotional with a quick prayer, song, and communion offered to any who'd not been there in the morning, break up into *work groups for the remaining 45 minutes*!
- For instance, at midweek services when the most-dedicated, hard-core, very knowledgeable members

gather---instead of having yet another Bible class similar to that which already took place on Sunday morning, have *midweek Bible Application Groups*!
- Or, for those members who are already quite familiar and expert in what the Bible teaches, instead of sitting and being lectured on passages already well-known to them---have *Sunday Morning Planning Groups*!

. . . . . . . . . . . . . . . . . . . . . . . . . . . . . . . . . . . . . . . . . . . . . . . . . . . . . . .

10) **Figure out how to get "small group" meaningful-discussion and work groups to function well** --- JESUS' MAIN MODE OF TEACHING AND MANAGEMENT WAS WITHIN A SMALL GROUP!

Yes, this does run counter to one of the severely-restrictive doctrines of some Church of Christ "splinter-groups": who sincerely feel that once the congregation has gathered together any "splitting of the body" into small groups is forbidden! I point this out because this severely-restrictive belief because it also is reflected in many of the mainline Church of Christ congregations: who fear small groups because the leadership might "lose control" of them.

A less-than righteous justification for avoiding small groups or even isolated classes (such as in place of the Sunday evening duplicate worship service) is to try and have the biggest audience for the preacher to deliver yet another sermon. Is the point of gathering together to hear yet one more sermon or lecture? Or is it to facilitate the work of the Lord? Is God an ego-maniac that needs us all to bow down in unison to him? Or is the "gathering together" of local Christians meant by the Lord to be a mechanism for *our* good, to facilitate our collective active growth?

Please remember that the best, most permanent, most meaningful "learning" is *not* from sitting passively hearing a lecture! It is when we engage directly on meaningful problems/opportunities---where my particular talents are exercised accomplishing important goals! That's where the very best learning occurs! This cannot happen in a large audience sitting passively in pews! For individual active engagement to occur, it needs to happen within a small-group environment.

Now some Church of Christ congregations in the past were intrigued by the success other Christian groups were having with "small groups" and decided to give it a shot. They designated areas of the town, host-houses, and told the people in that area to have house bible studies either Sunday evening or during the week. Almost invariably these efforts failed. Having given it a try that "crashed and burned," the leaders threw up their hands and said: "It doesn't work!" So they happily went back to the 'status-quo'!"

Having traditional mostly-lecture classes, or "Mickey-Mouse" children classes, or one-group sermons is easy. Breaking these into small-group study and work groups that function well is *HARD*! All sorts of procedural and interpersonal dynamics come into play that weren't relevant before! But it *can* work, evidenced by the number of other Christian groups using them to very good advantage: to attract visitors, energize established members, and interest their children!

For Small Groups to work they require: 1) expert continuing training of the key people involved; 2) strong continuing support by the leadership; and 3) a flexible format that appeals to your membership and the people of your community. None of this is easy. There are a thousand ways for the effort to easily "crash and burn." But without this component to your weekly church program it is highly unlikely you will be able to offer the close fellowship and personal involvement necessary to keep your present-day congregation viable.

Also, for those obsessed with "doing what the New Testament church did", small-group in-house weekly gatherings is clearly seen in the New Testament while "Christian church building" gatherings are *not*!

**Possible Action Items:**
- *Bring in some speakers* from congregations or other religious groups where Small Groups are functioning-well to give overviews of what they do.

- Actually *visit other congregations* or other religious groups where Small Groups are functioning-well to see firsthand how they make it work.
- *Read a book* --- there are many excellent, well-written, short books available at Amazon.com to order and have in your hands within a few days on the details of how to make Small Groups work.
- *Hold a series of Leadership meetings* with the only agenda item to discuss the relevancy, utility, and function options for Small Groups in your congregation (such as going through a key book together, chapter-by-chapter).
- *Pilot-test a possible format* with a test Small Group of people under your best guess at what will work for your congregation.
- After a few weeks *stop and evaluate what happened.* Expect to fail. Be determined to learn from the failures how to do better. Test the better format. Stop and evaluate. Continue until you have a format that functions well for your congregation and community.
- *Plan well in advance*: informing the congregation, explaining the value, training all the key participants, and pilot-testing before launching a congregation-wide Small Group effort.
- *Build a strong network of support* from other congregations or religious groups who are successful in Small Groups to help you with the inevitable problems and glitches.

........................................................

11) **Always combine "study" with application** --- JESUS WAS NOT SOME SCHOLAR LECTURING ON THE FINE POINTS OF ESOTERIC DOCTRINES SAFELY SEQUESTERED IN SOME SYNAGOGUE!

The greatest Doctrines in the world without meaningful Application are simply hot air ("faith without works is dead"). Likewise, to "just *do* something" without solidly-underpinning theory often results in disaster. Both must work "hand-in-glove" with each other to be successful: theory plus application!

Church of Christ congregations typically obsess on the theory while doing little or nothing on Application. In other words, Church of Christ congregations tend to stop at the "what?" without going on to the "how?" To be charitable, this is often not deliberate. Rather, this sad "short-changing" of the Example of Jesus is often structural rather than a conscious decision.

A good example of this is the monthly "men's business meeting" held by many mainline Church of Christ congregations. It has been my experience in faithfully attending these for many years that they are mostly a waste of time. Why? I see these structural problems: 1) too short a time-period allowed to get in meaningful discussion; 2) spiritually-trivial agenda items take up the time while "new business" is left to the last where there's usually no time for anything meaningful; 3) the important aspects of Christianity (versus the nuts-and-bolts of building management) are rarely brought up; 4) "Robert's Rules of Order" encourage factions to battle it out for getting the most votes versus building consensus; and 5) having put out an effort the men involved go away thinking that the "business" of the church has been met---while the weighty issues that Jesus insisted his followers deal with weren't talked about at all.

Another good example is the Sunday morning auditorium class. This is where rare visitors to the congregation would go. What they often get is just another sermon. At the last of the long lecture on some passage in the Bible the speaker will often ask: "Are there any questions?" Well, it's already past time to stop! Even if someone wanted to pursue deeper issues than the inevitable doctrines enumerated, there's no time! Certainly there's no time to take the scintillating Principles of Jesus that might be present in that text and consider *HOW* to implement such collectively! And when all four weekly time-periods unofficially mandated to be attended in order to be the "best" member are filled up with sermons, lectures, and discussions---the *STRUCTURE* prevents moving further!

Most people in our society can barely spare two time periods per week for church things, let alone four! Leadership needs to *MAKE A SPACE* for *DOING* together the teachings! Even if immediate activity is not warranted, at least refer to, describe, show by projection, or bring it up for discussion that such is being done in or out of the congregation: specific activity enlivening the vague generalities that the speaker is promoting!

Bring the vague generalities down to specifics and you may actually encourage others to *do* something with what you're teaching! And instead of just giving a passing nod, why not *GIVE EQUAL TIME* to Application vs. vague generalities on *everything* you teach! There is indeed a scripture in the Bible which explicitly states "Faith without Works is dead"! This translates to: "Knowledge without Application is useless." They are equal partners in Godliness. Make it so!

**Possible Action Items:**
- During the Sunday morning worship service, have *members give short reports on excellent activities* done within the congregation (to inform, inspire, and enlist yet other members);

- Don't insist on always having a full-length traditional sermon. Instead, *allow the speaker time to give reports* on activities in the congregation.
- *Have "special" business meetings* (in place of or in addition to the regular men's business meeting) where the only topic is an important desired or ongoing activity of the congregation.
- *Incorporate an activity component* into small-group Bible study mandates.
- *For every study topic* (whether chapter or verse or subject) identify a key "take-home message" for which that group will work on finding a way to actually turn it into a tangible result, either personally or collectively.
- *Bring in expert speakers on various desired activities* --- who will give focused, interesting presentations on things the congregation has a hand in or would like to do.
- *Provide the necessary time* for people to talk together, plan things, and continue to work on approved projects as part of the regular Church schedule (*not* "add-ons").

. . . . . . . . . . . . . . . . . . . . . . . . . . . . . . . . . . . . . . . . . . . . . . . . . . . . . . . .

12) **Instead of "milk" (vague-generality first-principles) concentrate on the "meat" of the Gospel (tangibly implementing the Radical Principles of Jesus)** --- JESUS ROSE ABOVE PETTY DEBATES TO HIGHER, RADICAL PRINCIPLES!

Whereas the Pharisees and scribes wished to trap Jesus into the minutiae of detailed debating, Jesus chose to rise above it all to address the obscured, underlying Principles. Jesus did not come to earth to make us into slightly-better debaters than our opponents! Instead, he came to sweep the rugs out from beneath our feet so that we could see the true "Firm Foundation" of the supporting floor!

First and foremost, Jesus put the emphasis back on God: *not* trivial doctrines, rituals, and ceremonies. Far superior to you being forced directly or indirectly by me to do things the way I (in my tiny little pea-brain) think will best honor God---is you truly honoring God in your heart by your actions towards others.

JESUS SPOKE CLEARLY AND PLAINLY ON THE TWO TOP PRIORITIES HIS FOLLOWERS SHOULD EMBRACE: 1) TO TRULY LOVE GOD ABOVE ALL ELSE; AND 2) TO EXTEND THAT GODLY LOVE TO OUR FELLOW, LITTLE, UNLOVBLE HUNMAN BEINGS.

It is so easy to get distracted on having the "right" doctrines and procedures that we forget the *purpose* to those doctrines and procedures! Hating those who deviate from what we feel is best in following God is to violate the second most important Principle from Jesus! If we fall back into hate then we can't truly love God!

This is where many religious leaders and followers on our little planet fail so miserably. They fervently preach that if a religious person "violates" this or that doctrine or procedure then those people are violating God, are at best "worshippers in error," and are at worst evil demons deliberating disrespecting God! As such, these "wrong-believers" are subject to being treated as the worst sort of demonic creatures---to be shunned, distained, raped, tortured, or murdered!

We see this behavior in present-day "religious radicals" across the world and are appalled! And yet the "splinter-group" Church of Christ congregations do not even talk to "mainline" Church of Christ congregations (and visa-versa) because they "worship in error"! And the mainline Church of Christ congregations do not even speak to the Baptist congregation that's literally on the other side of the street because *they* supposedly also "worship in error"!

Is this love? I think not. And since they cannot even talk to these other Christian people (because of the silly idea that talking to them would "fellowship" them, thus accepting their so-called "errors in belief and procedure"), cooperation on actually *DOING* the teachings of Jesus is out of the question! Once again, Doctrine trumps Principle.

Instead of focusing on Doctrine (which diverges and narrows with each traditionally-hardened generation, splintering into thousands of different "must-be-this-way" variations), why not focus on ways that actually work for implementing the Radical Principles of Jesus? Jesus' articulation of the two "greatest commandments" is only the start of a long list of amazingly-powerful Radical Principles!

These truly-Radical Principles are *not* easy, simple, or safe! Instead, they are difficult, complicated, and dangerous! So is it any wonder that people want to conveniently forget Jesus' scintillating Principles while lording it over their religious neighbors with their readily-executed, straight-forward, and non-threatening set of established procedures, exclusive doctrines, and often mindless ceremonies?

The "milk" of the Word is, indeed, tasty, fattening, and delicious. The "meat" is dangerous to obtain, hard to eat, and difficult to digest. But in the pursuit, cooking, and feasting---meat is far superior to milk. Babies drink exclusively milk. Men and women eat meat. As mature Christians we need to see the great Radical Principles of Jesus, consume them, incorporate them into our spiritual nature, and express them in our every thought, word, and action!

Is this hard? Damn right, it is! But it's also a wonderful challenge that offers us and our congregations true Transcendence rather than mere plodding boredom.

**Possible Action Items:**
- *Read through for yourself* Matthew, Mark, Luke, and John making a note at each of Jesus' actions and teachings as to what Principle he is advocating and/or illustrating.
- Instead of just defending some simple doctrine in a sermon or class, ask: *"What is the Principle being taught here?"*
- Ask the question: *"HOW might we implement this great Principle* from Jesus today, here, for the people of our community?"
- *Do not limit your thinking/discussion* to the procedures and doctrines handed down to you from prior generations within your existing religious Tradition. Truly grasp and use the enabling Freedom which Jesus gave to you!

13) **Believe Jesus when he explicitly stated which people would make it into heaven; and help the congregation to *be* those people** --- JESUS CLEARLY STATED THE TOP CRITERIA THAT WOULD SEPARATE THE "SHEEP" FROM THE "GOATS" ON THE DAY OF JUDGMENT!

Only days before the religious leaders of his time succeeded in having Jesus crucified, He told His followers who would make it into heaven on the Day of Judgment.

Was it all those who dutifully met at the local church building four times per week? Was it all those who sat through thousands of sermons on topics where they already knew the take-home messages perfectly well? Was it for all those who went over the same scriptures in Bible classes hundreds of times? Was it for those that got all the doctrines and beliefs "right"? No.

Jesus said that those who would be accepted by God into heaven at the Day of Judgment were those who implemented the Radical Principles of Godliness by helping their fellow man in times of need. Should not this be a congregation's top priority? Sadly, it is clearly *not* the top priority of most mainline Church of Christ congregations.

In fact, many Church of Christ congregations operate largely divorced from their community. They do not interact with other Christian groups. They rarely do anything helpful to the members of their community. They only reluctantly part with a few "benevolence" dollars if someone comes to the building and begs for help. Instead, they---to all appearances---strive to be the "intellectuals" of Christianity who spend most of their collective time preaching, lecturing, and reading the Bible.

Is this what Jesus explicitly stated would get people into heaven? No! Of course there's nothing wrong with preaching, lecturing, and reading of the Bible. But JESUS WAS SO FOCUSED ON THE KEY GODLY PRINCIPLES THAT HE DID NOT EVEN LEAVE BEHIND ANY WRITTEN MANDATES! It was left to later disciples after his death to write down some of what he'd taught and done!

Yes, the Bible as a whole is a critical "operator's manual" for righteousness and Godliness. But once having gotten the key "take-home messages" from an operational manual, do you then obsessively keep studying it over and over? No! You *implement* the instructions to gain skill and mastery at *using* the equipment! Sure, you refer back to the manual now and then to make sure you're on track or if some unexpected problem arises. But the point is to *USE* the Manual to *OPERATE* the provided equipment!

Jesus in the very last days of His time on earth struck to the very heart of his Teachings to set the top priorities for his hard-headed, tradition-bound disciples! *"Express your Love to God by extending that same love to your fellow men and women in tangible ways that help them with their valid needs!"*

Some Christian churches do this quite successfully! This *is* possible to do not just individually but collectively! Mainline Church of Christ congregations need to *MAKE TIME* in their weekly schedule to *DO* the *TOP PRIORITY* for them getting into heaven! Don't you think so?

**Possible Action Items:**
- Change the weekly Wednesday night Bible Study into an evening for *Bible Application Groups*: where like-minded and talented people each week spend at least 45 minutes in small groups (after a 15 minute devotional where all are gathered together before going to their various work groups) pooling their talents planning, testing, and implementing programs aimed at helping people in need. *A GREAT DEAL CAN BE*

*ACCOMPLISHED IN A YEAR BY HIGHLY-TALENTED PEOPLE WORKING FOR JUST A FEW MINUTES TOGETHER EACH AND EVERY WEEK!*

- In order to implement the above change to the weekly schedule, first you need to *identify people with particular interest/talents* in each of the major areas of church service. It can be as easy as sending out a short questionnaire or as complicated as using an online "spiritual gifts evaluation."
- *The appointed Leadership specifically endorses and mandates* the various Bible Application groups---as well as approving specific plans from the groups.
- *Leadership provides ongoing training, oversight, necessary resources, and continued encouragement.*
- As another good option, the same thing can be done for selected people who are past the point of needing additional sermons or detailed Bible classes on *either Sunday morning during the "Bible class" period or during the Sunday evenings duplicate worship period.*
- *Note that young people will benefit from being part of this active group effort* as much or more than the adults.

---

## Chapter Three:

# DOCTRINE

14) **In your doctrine, truly put "first things" first** --- JESUS CLEARLY STATED WHAT SHOULD BE HIS FOLLOWER'S TOP TWO DOCTRINAL PRIORITIES!

Let your main Doctrine be to collectively implement the Radical Principles of Jesus!

The Church of Christ notion of the greatest service to God, which will make the Creator of the Universe the happiest with us, is to sit being lectured at on things from the Bible that they already know while following all the exact dictates of handed-down Tradition. Yes, this is indeed a painful chore for matured Christians already quite familiar with the take-home messages of the Bible and for whom the rituals have been done so many times they are virtually meaningless. But Jesus did not order the many thousands coming out to his events to return to their synagogues to dutifully be lectured on the life of Abraham for yet the thousandth time!

Group meetings are valuable, particularly for facilitating people of like interest and talents to productively work together. But THE FOCUS SHOULD BE ON WHAT JESUS STATED THE MAIN FOCUS SHOULD BE: 1) LOVING GOD WITH ALL OUR HEARTS, MINDS, AND SOULS; AND 2) EXTENDING THE LOVE OF GOD TO OTHER HUMANS.

How do we best accomplish these objectives? Is it by spending all our "church" time isolated from our communities preaching/lecturing at each other on things we already know? Surely, it is not.

Change your Doctrine into the Radical Principles of Jesus and you will transform your congregation! It will replace "boring" with *exciting*! It will replace "nothing tangible achieved" with *productivity*! It will replace "painful duty" with *growth*! It will replace "endless repetition" with *true learning*!

**Possible Action Items:**
- *Teach Jesus' Radical Principles first* and other doctrines second.
- *Incorporate examples* of people actually striving to implement Jesus' Radical Principles.
- *Give updates* on how people in your congregation are actually striving to DO the Radical Principles of Christ.

. . . . . . . . . . . . . . . . . . . . . . . . . . . . . . . . . . . . . . . . . . . . . . . . . . . . .

15) **Forget about being so-called religious "conservatives", "moderates", or "liberals" and instead become Jesus-Radicals** --- JESUS WAS NOT A CONSERVATIVE, MODERATE, OR LIBERAL.  INSTEAD, HE WAS A RADICAL!

From the beginning of mankind's spiritual development, conservatives have fought with liberals.  This is illustrated in the very first book of the Bible.  Both Cain and Able sought to be pleasing to God by offering Him acceptable burnt-sacrifices.  Cain was the conservative who kept within the close boundaries, tending the home fires, and growing crops.  Able was the liberal who wandered far away, herding a flock of animals, finding them pasture where-ever.

When it came time to sacrifice to God, Cain offered crops as his burnt offering.  Able offered up the best of his flock.  God favored Able, the liberal, who was then killed by his more-conservative brother in a fit of anger and jealousy.  So it is today.

Every church "split" I've ever seen had at its roots conservatives fighting with liberals.  Should we be conservatives that value Tradition over Progress?  Should be liberals who favor Progress over Tradition?  Or should we "reasonably" compromise and be Moderates who will accept a little Progress if it doesn't mean changing Tradition too much?

I suggest we forget about all of that and instead be *Jesus Radicals*!  By this I do not mean we that should take up weapons to drive-down, subjugate, and/or destroy anyone who doesn't agree with our traditional beliefs, doctrines, and procedures---as do many radicals in the religious world today!  Neither do I mean the opposite: being zealots who take up arms to fight with, conquer, or leave behind those who don't readily reject the old to embrace the new!  Rather, I strongly urge the mainline Church of Christ to embrace the Radical Principles of Jesus as their proclaimed Doctrine!

If you were to fully embrace the #2 Radical Principle of Jesus to "love other people as yourself" what would this mean for the poor, the sick, and the downtrodden of your community? How much of your collective church effort would shift from sermons and lectures to fulfilling this mandate? No, this is not just a duty of individual Christians, as Church of Christ doctrine tries to insinuate, thus protecting its sermon and lecture times!

You cannot burn up all your church time together being "intellectual", or just give a token effort now and then, to properly fulfill a #2 top priority of Christianity! Indeed, this is your #2 *DUTY*! Nothing other than truly loving God is greater---and that #1 doctrine is made-manifest by the second! So let your Radical nature be expressed by your *ACTIVE LOVE* to other people! Let this be your greatest, most-important Doctrine! Teach it!

And more than teaching the vague generality---teach *HOW* to actually do it: by demonstration, example, and well-supported participation! Learn and teach effective methods, techniques, and procedures for loving other people as if they were you.

Other Christian groups do it! Other Christian groups are famous for their choosing this as their #2 Doctrine! Why can't you do the same? The answer is that traditional doctrine trumps Jesus' Principles. Really? Why can't Jesus' Principles come first?

**Possible Action Items:**
- *Inventory* the needs of your community.
- *Select* what valid needs your congregation might help address.
- *Study* as to effective methods that work in your area for addressing the identified needs.

- *Teach people the techniques and procedures needed to address the needs.*
- *Preach and discuss the Biblical examples and rationale for implementing the Radical Principles* of Jesus which support your approach to meeting the identified community needs.
- *Link the efforts directly to Jesus*: providing prayers, Bible reading, singing, and verse-discussion as a required part of people in your community receiving help from the congregation.
- *Evangelize others by incorporating them into your helpful actions.*
- *Let the community vividly SEE your Doctrine* by your collective, congregational, interactive Actions.

. . . . . . . . . . . . . . . . . . . . . . . . . . . . . . . . . . . . . . . . . . . . . . . . . . .

16) **Stop being proud of supposedly being better than others** --- JESUS EXCORIATED RELIGIOUS HYPOCRITES WHO THOUGHT THEY WERE HOLIER THAN OTHERS.

Although Church of Christ congregations do have a doctrine of humility, it is not perceived that way by others. Insisting that they have "The Truth" in all matters, Church of Christ congregations typically radiate a haughty arrogance. Furthermore, being "God's true children" while others are at best "worshipping in error" engenders a great Pride that is entirely *un*-Christ-like.

Yes, this is not exclusive to Church of Christ members. Most religious groups feel that they are "God's true followers" doing everything in the best way possible: having the best beliefs, the best doctrines, the best rituals, and the best ceremonies. However, other groups do not necessarily judge others as "wrong" just because they are different!

Church of Christ members have been brought up from babies believing that anything different from what they believe and do is automatically wrong. This is reflected in the Church of Christ feeble efforts at local, personal evangelism: instead of showing people Jesus they are taught to argue doctrine. Somehow, preachers of the Church of Christ think that offering a slightly-better doctrine than the group next door will cause people to flock into the doors! Wrong.

People don't care about doctrine. They don't see that the Church of Christ is any better or different from that other group across the street. What they care about is whether or not you are willing to make a personal connection with them seeing them as a valuable individual, not as merely another soul to be "saved" by baptism conducted in the proper manner.

Instead of pride, try *GRATITUDE*! We can look at the positives in our religious congregations and be thankful we are fortunate enough to have them! Then, we can offer what we have to others not as vague generalities, or confusing doctrines, or "absolute" mandates---but through our sincere and effective help in matters that others agree are useful to them!

Yes, preaching at people from a pulpit in our comfortable church building is easy. Standing down from the pulpit to go out onto the street and help others like-unto ourselves overcome severe problems is hard.

Once again, folks, few of us have the talents to do this by ourselves! It has to be a collective effort where all our various talents support each other in well-constructed programs. By our helpful actions people will judge us, not by our condemning rhetoric.

**Possible Action Items:**
- In sermons, use *examples of Christians effectively helping others* as key illustrations versus just mouthing vague generalities.
- Instead of insisting things are "right" or "wrong" *consciously substitute "best"*.
- *Talk to the other religious group across the street*! Even contemplate joint activities where you pool your resources to do great things for your community!
- *Join cross-denominational groups* in your community.
- Rather than evangelize by arguing doctrine, *evangelize by offering Jesus-linked effective help* to people in need!
- *Do Bible Class discussion of "gray" areas* and questions where there isn't a necessarily "right" or "wrong" answer! (i.e. "Why?" and "How?"-type questions).

..............................................................

17) **Forget about feeling superior to other religious groups because you have "the Truth" while they do not** --- JESUS WELCOMED BOTH "SINNERS" AND "HERETICS" TO HIS EVENTS!

Instead of trying to convert people, focus on offering them effective Jesus-linked help to their problems. When they see your sincere, tangibly-helpful actions they will see Jesus. Welcome them into your active Christian community.

Focusing on condemning others as "sinners" or "heretics" will only drive them away. Allow God to be the supreme Judge. Instead of judging people, strive to help them. Instead of trying to save people, show them Jesus in your congregation's activities. Invite them to be part of your obviously-worthy efforts.

The religious leaders of Jesus' time greatly faulted him for allowing those thrown out of the synagogues to attend his events. The religious leadership was even more outraged when Jesus associated with proven sinners! But Jesus was more concerned with people as God's wayward children needing help than in proving he was morally and religiously superior to them!

As Jesus did, we also can focus on encouraging and growing the Good rather than condemning the Evil. Ranting against "sin" is easy. Nurturing and growing the good that's present in all people is a difficult, tricky, and even dangerous challenge! Once again, few of us individuals have in ourselves all the varied skills and talents necessary to do this on our own. To be effective, we need to pool our talents in well-managed, well-constructed, ongoing programs. This puts an even heavier burden on church leadership to be Godly Wise Managers and Quality Leaders.

Have as our official doctrine that we are *all* sinners unworthy of Salvation---all of us needing the continuing Grace of God to be saved!  Have as our official doctrine that *"the Truth" is only viable when it is EXPRESSED AS TANGIBLE OUTCOMES!*  Faith without works is dead!

Express our Truth by people seeing and agreeing that we as a group are actively implementing the teachings of Jesus!  Always wish other people the best while demonstrating to them the open arms of Jesus.

**Possible Action Items:**
- In sermons, lecture, and discussions instead of delighting in condemning sin *obsess on promoting and building-up the good.*
- *Create welcoming activities* at your church that others might be interested in attending: such as instead of just "come to Bible study" (which few have any interest in) offer wonderful concerts, community meals, holiday celebrations, meeting unmet needs, etc.---all directly tied to Jesus.
- *Connect with the other religious groups* in your community in a positive fashion: such as joining in occasional cross-the-board religious community events.
- *Offer specific programs that help sinners* in ways that they will agree are helpful --- such as marriage-trouble counseling, grief recovery groups, addiction cessation maintenance, debt counseling, anger management, etc.  Once again, this requires specialized training, skill, and even certification.  Consider bringing in established counselors or groups specializing in those areas to partner with the church while always linking the help to Jesus and your congregation.
- *Study/present books/films/videos etc. other than the Bible* which will intrigue people to participate---while always linking those back to the Bible.  This could be as simple as a "Christian Book Club" that reads selected Christian-themed books---or as complicated as a Film Series where actual Hollywood films are shown

(not just amateurish Bible-doctrine films) which are then discussed in relation to key passages in the Bible.

..................................................

18) **Consider returning to the historical Church of Christ's doctrinal roots** --- JESUS WAS NOT OBSESSED WITH GETTING THE PREVAILING JEWISH DOCTRINES "RIGHT" BUT IN OPENING PEOPLE'S HEARTS TO GOD!

The historical movement that resulted in the Church of Christ began in the 1800's. It was in response to the increasingly-bitter fighting amongst the protestant groups as to who had the "right" doctrines. In reaction to the increasingly-detailed creeds of the various groups, several prominent preachers proposed trashing them all and falling back on a revolutionary concept encapsulated in the slogan: *"Where the Bible speaks we'll speak; and where it is silent we will be silent."*

As to what it means to speak where the Bible speaks, a second key slogan crisply summarized: *"One Lord, one Faith, one Baptism; and in everything else, Love."* This meant that even though people had many differences over the many details of Christianity, people would agree to respect each other as intelligent people coming to their own meaningful conclusions for their own lives in matters not essential to salvation.

These two slogans were a breath of fresh air in an increasingly-bitter, acrid religious environment. In reaction, for a short period of time, the Church of Christ movement was the fastest growing religious group in the United States.

However, it is human nature to want "the" answer, the "right" position, and the accepted "Truth"---on everything! Having a set, detailed, concrete Doctrine is simple, easy, and safe. Letting the other person come to his or her own conclusions different from me is complicated, difficult, and dangerous.

And so within a few decades the Church of Christ movement resulted in such a restrictive doctrine, exclusive procedures, and repetitive rituals that the founders of the movement were likely groaning in their graves.  The Church of Christ had become one of the worst examples of that which it originally rebelled against.

However, its grand-though-naïve beginning could help save the present Church of Christ if only its members would embrace their original, refreshing doctrine.

By adopting RESPECT for each other and others---while not at all having to give up or compromise one's own beliefs---would allow "theological space" to do as I've strongly suggested in previous points: 1) put Jesus' Radical Principles in place of traditional doctrine; 2) promote the Good rather than obsessing on condemning the Bad; and 3) substitute effective Action for preaching and lecturing.

**Possible Action Items:**
- *Resurrect the two initial Church of Christ slogans.* Explain them.  Put them up on the walls, on the stationary, on one's church sign.  Use them to free up intellectual and actual church space and time for Principles, Good, and Action.
- *Actively fellowship the other Church of Christ congregations* in your area---whether "splinter," "liberal," or "conservative."  Call them up on the phone.  Sit down with their leaders in person.  Talk to them.  Explore where you might cooperate to further the cause of bringing people to Christ in your community.
- *Instead of being exclusionary, be inclusive.*  Welcome people with different religious backgrounds.   Of course teach One Lord, One Faith, and One Baptism.  But in everything else allow people to come to their own good conclusions rather than insisting on the one "right" answer.

..............................................................

19) **Change your doctrinal mandate from "protect the Truth" to "*DO the Truth*"** --- JESUS DEMONSTRATED HOW TO TURN HIS RADICAL TEACHINGS INTO TANGIBLE ACTIVITY!

Jesus was not just a mouth from which poured amazing lectures. Jesus did not only say: "Just believe what I've taught you." Instead, Jesus was an *EXAMPLE* of *HOW* to turn his Radical Principles into real, tangible action! IN REPLY TO THOSE WHO QUESTIONED THE VALIDITY OF WHAT HE TAUGHT, JESUS SAID TO LOOK AT HIS ACTIONS!

Think about the pinnacle of his life and teachings: the Cross. His Radical Teachings culminated in him giving his life, allowing his enemies to torture him to death on the cross. Indeed, his explicit decree was that anyone who wished to follow him *MUST* pick up their *own* crosses and follow in his bloody footsteps! That, my friend, is not theory. It is Action.

JESUS IN THE MANY OTHER EVENTS AND CIRCUMSTANCES OF HIS LIFE, AS DETAILED IN THE GOSPELS, PUT HIS OWN WORDS INTO ACTION---SHOWING US HOW TO DO THEM!

Indeed, the point was not to have an intellectual discussion on the fine points of theological writings---but to incorporate them into our minds by meaningful, targeted, productive actions!

To truly follow Jesus we, his modern-day disciples, *MUST WALK IN HIS FOOTSTEPS*... not just figuratively, but literally! In facing any problem or opportunity, we as his disciples must ask: "What did Jesus do in similar circumstance?" And "How can I---in my own little way, in my own present-day situation---do similar?"

Your youth, your confirmed members, and your visitors are not just listening to your rhetoric---they are watching your actions! Are we today just like everyone else with a thin veneer of religiosity covering up our smart-animal selfishness? Or do we really believe in Jesus?

If we really believe in Jesus then our goal is to think like him, look like him, and act like him! Faith without works is dead! You can have the "best" doctrine, the "finest" rituals, and the "most-correct' beliefs in the world---and have it all be useless! It won't keep your young people from leaving. It won't stop your back-benchers from slipping out the door. It won't attract new people to your congregation.

"The" Truth must be demonstrated by Action! The Action that works is based on the rebellious, Principle-driven, Radical Jesus! Jesus adapted his Message and Actions to the time and place of the society and people he encountered. We must be flexible enough to do the same!

"Protect the Truth" is just an excuse to take the easy way out: to fall back on traditional beliefs and procedures whether or not they are effective in helping people come to God in our present-day world. "Protect the Truth" is the *wrong* mandate for serious Christians!

Indeed, the religious leaders of Jesus' time were loudly proclaiming that very imperative as they happily butchered Jesus! "*Do* the Truth!" is an *AIM* that can change everything. Suddenly we have to think "*HOW*"? Suddenly we have to make things actually work, not just blame people for being bad when inherited techniques, procedures, and doctrines fail. Suddenly we have to find ways to change abstract beliefs into concrete Actions.

Yes, this is by far a more complicated, difficult, and dangerous path than deifying the Status Quo. Concentrating on effective action is far more likely to be more enjoyable and productive than stagnation. Concentrating on putting our beliefs into productive action is better than sitting silently on a pew watching your congregation die.

**Possible Action Items:**
- *Preachers do not stop at vague generalities.* Conclude sermons with "How to we then do this?" Give inspiring outside examples and actual things going on within the congregation, to which others can join if they wish.
- In sermons, lectures, and discussion classes *give equal weight to Jesus' Actions along with his words.* Then ask the question: "How might we today do similar?"
- *Re-evaluate everything your congregation does* in regards to: "Is this procedure meeting its objective?' If not, consider improvements or replacement with something else that has a better chance to meet that objective.
- *Take realistic stock of your congregation's resources, especially the talents of your people.* Unfortunately, most Church of Christ congregations don't even know what backgrounds, skills, and talents exist in its membership. Send out a survey, do in-house interviews, and start a computer-based searchable system.
- *Don't just impose things from above.* Instead, engage all your people in suggesting directions, priorities, and activities to meet clearly-defined objectives.
- *Make "DO THE TRUTH" a motto* that's put on the walls, taught in classes, printed on the church stationary, and is painted on the sign in front of the building.

## Chapter Four:

# EVANGELISM

20) **Employ a "friendship evangelism" program for the congregation: building strong Christian relationships through meaningful service mutually discovering helpful Principles within enjoyable sacrifice** --- JESUS CONVERTED PEOPLE TO HIS CAUSE BY OFFERING GODLY FRIENDSHIP: WHERE ACTIVE SERVICE FACILITATED DISCOVERY OF HELPFUL PRINCIPLES CHALLENGING EACH PERSON TO MUTUALLY-TRANSCENDENT, ENJOYABLE SACRIFICE!

In the Church of Christ, evangelism is often seen (whether consciously or not) as converting people to the traditional doctrine of the Church of Christ. This mainly involves people getting baptized in the proper manner, then faithfully sitting in Worship services being preached at---plus sitting in Bible classes being lectured at---for the rest of your life.

This is a very poor version of Christianity. Following Jesus is not summed up by claiming to not be a denomination. Following Jesus is not summed up by claiming to be the "true" church that goes back to the New Testament. This form of "Christianity" is a poor reflection composed almost entirely of doctrine and procedure. JESUS ROSE ABOVE DOCTRINE AND PROCEDURE.

The things that truly convert (change) a person from a casual sinner to a God-loving righteous person are the same now as it was for the people in New Testament times, namely: 1) offering true friendship, 2) proven by actively helping with people with their immediate needs, in which we are 3) willing to sacrifice our own pleasure to elevate others. Jesus did this.

ON A PERSONAL AND COLLECTIVE LEVEL, JESUS OFFERED TRUE FRIENDSHIP PROVEN BY ACTIVELY HELPING PEOPLE WITH THEIR IMMEDIATE NEEDS BY SACRIFICING HIS OWN PLEASURE TO ELEVATE OTHERS!

Arguing doctrine is easy: "I'm right and you are wrong!" Engaging with people on a personal level, in a helpful way, targeting their specific needs, willing to go beyond our comfort zones for them...is hard! It is complicated. It is even a bit dangerous! But it is what you would do for a real friend!

"Friendship" evangelism doesn't go bother strangers. It focuses on people who are already our acquaintances, relatives, and neighbors. Once again, few of us have all the different talents necessary in order to broach religious topics in a positive manner to which people will respond! In order to be effective, "friendship evangelism" requires a solid, well-supported, ongoing program involving a variety of people with a variety of talents.

Church of Christ preachers typically beat up individual people for not somehow doing all the many things themselves necessary for having an effective evangelistic program. Such preaching is counter-productive. People silently look back up at the pontificating speaker on his pulpit "soapbox" and think: "Now, this gentleman is the most-talented amongst us---and what is *his* track-record at doing what he's saying we should do?"

It is not unusual for that pontificating preacher to have zero home Bible studies going on, have few if any baptisms during the past year, and have little contact with people outside the congregation. And he's presumably the *most* talented person in the congregation in terms of Bible knowledge, interaction skills, and presentation technique!

If asked about his own track-record, he will typically fall back on the standard excuse: "I don't have the time to go out and make contacts since I'm putting together all these sermons and lecture classes, doing ministry work with the sick and such, and keeping up with my own Bible study!" It's a feeble excuse---and yet he does have a point.

In today's disconnected, hectic, highly-prioritized society it is difficult to make and nourish meaningful personal contacts. Thus the age of "door-knocking" to find interested people is over, at least in the Western, developed societies. But those with whom we already have meaningful contact might be interested in developing a closer relationship with God if it is offered in a context they find compelling.

JESUS OFFERED CLOSER RELATIONSHIP TO GOD WITHIN A CONTEXT THAT THE PEOPLE FOUND COMPELLING: OFFERING PEOPLE WHAT THEY PERCEIVED AS REAL BENEFITS THAT MET THEIR TRUE NEEDS!

Jesus met their true needs by offering the people: 1) *healing* of their physical ills when the "medicine" of his age could do no more for them; 2) *food* for their hungry bellies; 3) religious *respect* when the Synagogues would not accept them or had kicked them out; 4) interesting sermons offering *new insights* as illustrated by powerful examples from their present-day life; 5) *radical Principles* that challenged them to transform their own hearts; 6) a *compelling AIM* tied to the single greatest Problem of their society; and 7) Jesus and His disciples' *loving friendship*!

If we could do all this today it would have the same evangelistic results as did Jesus 2,000 years ago---because our deepest spiritual needs are the same today as they were then! However, doing "all of the above" is indeed complicated, difficult, and even dangerous!

The "status quo" of mainline Church of Christ congregations is clearly *not* succeeding at offering the above to its youth, to visitors, or even to its own members. Emulating Jesus' evangelistic efforts today would be far beyond just "talking to people about Jesus" as preachers insist we can all do! It requires us to pool our talents together in an organized, well-structured, well-supported congregational "friendship evangelism" program.

*Lacking this, you Preachers and other Church Leaders please stop beating up your members for "not talking to others about Jesus" enough!*

I well remember when, in seeking authoritative endorsements, I sent a book I'd written on friendship evangelism to one of the Church of Christ acclaimed overall Leaders. The reply I received back was that the system I proposed in my book was too complicated for the average congregation to implement.

On the one hand, that was an outrageous insult to the very skilled, talented, and dedicated Christians I've seen in all the congregations of which I've been part! Are you seriously telling me that people in the average congregation are unable to do the following steps: 1) ask the congregation to identify possible people for visits; 2) prioritize according to Bible standards who to visit first; 3) phone for appointments; 4) have expert, trained teams visit with the people; 5) in a very casual and friendly way find out more about them, while telling them about the local congregation, offering them personal in-home Bible studies if they wish; 6) jot down the results on a file card; and 7) filing the cards alphabetically or datewise in a box? Yes, this did not even require some complicated computer program, just file cards and boxes (this was some years ago).

But, sadly, on the other hand, such simple things *are* indeed beyond the capability of most of the Church of Christ *leader-*

*ships* that I've encountered over the years (for reasons discussed in further points).

Preachers love to beat their flocks up for not bringing their friends to church---and yet often can't even put into play a simple, effective, visitation program!

Of course an effective visitation program is just a start. You have to have something to bring interested people to that they will see is of real value to them for meeting their valid needs.

For that to happen---in parallel to a strong, effective visitation program---you first must identify the valid needs of the community that your congregation can help meet, establish programs to do such in an effective manner, and tie it all strongly back to Jesus and God. Then, when combined with a visitor-friendly, well-constructed, and well-executed program at the Sunday morning church service (tied to small-group, in-home discussion studies)---you just might have a shot at an actual, effective evangelistic effort!

**Possible Action Items:**
- Establish an ongoing, effective, *visitation program*.
- Make sure you have a *visitor-friendly, impactful Sunday morning service*.
- Have ongoing *small-group, home-study Bible fellowships* in place.
- Have people capable of giving *individual New Testament Bible discussion* sessions in the people's own homes, should they wish.
- Have a *strong support system* in place to nurture and support new converts.
- Quickly involve interested new people not just in theoretical Bible study but in actual *work-group application* thereto.

21) **Stop thinking that lecturing people is the best way to teach them** --- JESUS' MAIN MODE OF TEACHING WAS O.J.T. "ON-THE-JOB-TRAINING"!

A key point of my book "In Search of Quality: Principles and Mechanisms" is how to deliver *effective* instruction! Many good-hearted, sincere people in the Church of Christ consider themselves to be good teachers...but it's common that after a few hours or days following the sermon or class that the audience or members of that class have no memory at all of what was covered!

Yes, those people were fervently lectured-at or preach-to. But how is that *effective* teaching? Short answer: it wasn't.

In my book I make the following points on this subject: 1) the *least* effective mode of teaching is an unadorned, monologue sermon or lecture; 2) *seeing* the lesson (such as adding the projection of interesting images or video) is ten times as effective as a monologue lecture; 3) *Direct involvement* (such as participation by the students in meaningful discussion) is ten times more effective than visuals; and 4) ten times more effective than even direct involvement is O.J.T. "On The Job Training." O.J.T. is applying knowledge to real tasks of real value to real people. This is what I call the "teaching-effectiveness curve."

O.J.T. is the main way that Jesus instructed his closest disciples. Yes, "lecturing," "seeing," and "discussion" all had their places. But Jesus quickly moved on to the *most* effective training by involving his disciples in directly applying his teachings doing real tasks of real value to real people!

At your job---where your reputation, livelihood, and self-esteem hang in the balance---directly applying theory to important tasks causes meaningful knowledge to be quickly "burned" into your brain and muscles! You don't have to think about it anymore. You know it! It's part of you!

Consider mastering some new computer program at your workstation. Let's say it's a photo-enhancement program totally new to you. You have no idea how to work or use this program. For your training, your boss might send you to a general lecture on how various photo-enhancement programs work. Ok. Now you have a general awareness. Or, your boss might bring in a speaker to give a slide presentation to your entire office on how this program works. Fine, now you've got a vague awareness of how the program works. Or your boss might send you to a small class with computer terminals where each person gets to actually work with the program, ask questions, and get direct help on how to use the program. This is great! Now you know everything you need to know, right? Now you're an expert on this program, right? Not at all...going back to your own desk at work with specific assignments in front of you, you're still confused and bewildered. If your boss were really smart, he or she would simply bring the instructor into the office for a week to be on call, ready to come and sit with you struggling with your particular assignment. The very best of all would be to move as quickly as possible to the O.J.T. itself---where you get the most effective learning by directly applying the knowledge to the important task.

This Principle works. It works in the military (famous for its effective teaching via O.J.T.), in business settings, in schools, and even in religion! Some religious groups do this quite well. Unfortunately, Church of Christ congregations spend most of their time at the *least* effective level of teaching. Is it any wonder that "learning" is rudimentary if at all?

But---once again---it's quite easy to give a lecture. It's hard, complicated, and even dangerous to take key information to the level of an individual attempting to use it with real "customers." Just as in the business example I gave, it takes wise Quality managers that understand effective teaching, know how and where to give key help, have a clear view of what needs to be achieved, provide the critical support without which it won't work, and supply the solid framework (program) within which it all holds-together.

Also, please note that it is easy to "game" this Radical Principle of "Learning by Doing." Every congregation I've ever been part of has a sprinkling of activities which on paper look great! Some of these activities indeed are quite meaningful and substantial. Many of them, however, involve few or just one person, are only done rarely, or exist only in the paper description!

The point is not to "do things" but to actually *TEACH* in the *best* way---through Application! Why? Because teaching through Application is *THE MOST EFFECTIVE MEANS* by which you can intrigue, energize, and enthuse your youth, your visitors, and your members.

Another defense for falling back on the easiest and least-effective modes of teaching is: "But we can't get the people to do anything! They just want to come and sit in the pews! I've tried to get them to do things, but they won't!"

Please listen closely. "Make work" will not work. People will just ignore it. "Trivial work" (common to Church of Christ activities) doesn't teach anything. People will plod through it then leave. To get enthusiastic, continuing involvement congregational Applications have to be the following: 1) meaningful, 2) interesting to all involved, 3) personal growth-promoting, 4) customer-oriented, 5) strongly leadership-supported, 6) combine mutually-helpful various talents of various people, and 7) synergistic (where the results are greater than any single person alone could achieve).

"But," you might respond, "that which you describe is complicated, difficult, and dangerous!" Yes. It's what Jesus did for his disciples---and what you as Church leaders need to also provide for your membership.

**Possible Action Items:**
- Give sermons and lectures that *include powerful, impactful visual slide and/or video components.*
- Tie Sunday morning sermons to *meaningful discussion questions* (for which there are no "right" or "wrong" answers) which are the main theme of small group weekly meetings of the membership.
- Always provide specific, *recommended "Action Items"* in sermons, lectures, and discussion classes, which people can implement on their own or be part of ongoing efforts should they wish.
- Encourage your people by various effective means to *come up with their own suggested Action Items* for Leadership evaluation and approval (a key question in discussion classes and groups; and from specifically-endorsed committees; and from ongoing Work Groups composed of mutually-interested people).
- *Show-case your congregation's application* of Bible teachings (such as brief 5 or 10-minute updates on various projects and programs during Sunday morning or other meetings; or articles in mail-outs; or praise in bulletins).
- *Bring in invited speakers/presenters* on inspiring activities outside the congregation that you either support or wish to implement yourselves.
- *Make "Do the Truth" an explicit slogan* that you put on your stationary, at the top of your bulletin, hung up on the walls, and painted on your sign in front of your building.

. . . . . . . . . . . . . . . . . . . . . . . . . . . . . . . . . . . . . . . . . . . . . . . . . . . . . . . . . .

22) **Stop thinking that lecturing people on doctrine is the best way to convert them to Jesus** --- JESUS PROVIDED HIS FOLLOWERS WITH THE BEST WAY TO CONVERT OTHERS TO HIS TEACHINGS: DIRECTLY INVOLVE THEM IN APPLYING HIS TEACHINGS!

A picture is worth a thousand words. Your example is worth a thousand pictures. Involving others in your efforts is worth a thousand of your example. So---assuming my calculations are correct---your involving another person in active application together with you is *A BILLION TIMES MORE EFFECTIVE* than just standing up giving them a lecture on the topic! Rather staggering, don't you think? Are you interested in "teaching the Gospel" or "*effectively* teaching the Gospel"?

Let me give you a very sad example. A couple came to church. A person who fancied himself a preacher (he'd graduated from a preaching school) went with me and some other people to "teach" them in their home. He was an "assistant minister" and took the lead. He pointed out various verses in the Bible, reading them himself, and lecturing them on how they collectively taught a person to "hear, believe, repent, confess, and be baptized." The couple dutifully came down to the church building again, and was baptized. Then they continued on as faithful, diligent, interested members...for two or three weeks! Then we never saw them again.

Were they taught? Yes. Were they taught *effectively*? No. By no stretch of the imagination were they taught Jesus. They were taught doctrine. Even though they were persuaded to follow the doctrine (mainly through fear of going to hell if they didn't), it was not near enough to get them to stay with the church.

If people were first and foremost really taught Jesus, then there'd be no problem at all with doctrines such as baptism. A conviction to become a disciple of Jesus makes a person try to do everything Jesus taught, particularly to be baptized. "Hey, here's water! What is there to stop me from being baptized right now!?"

And yet the "intellectual" Church of Christ approach is to obsess on the doctrine while forgetting Jesus. Is it any wonder that people are not knocking down the church building's doors in their eagerness to come in?

Even sadder is the typical sermon in the Church of Christ. Not only is it focused on "first-principle" doctrine ("Believe in God"... "obey God"... "believe in Jesus"... "you must be baptized" ... "there's only one church" ... "You have to attend services"... "our procedures are the correct ones" etc.)---but it's repeatedly delivered to people who *already* know it, *already* accept it, and have *already* heard it many times before!

Thus it becomes not only ineffective in "teaching," but it is *de*-motivating! And, this "you're so dumb I have to keep repeating the simplest things to you because otherwise you'd forget" paternalistic, insulting attitude extends not just to sermons but Bible classes.

It's like I overheard yesterday right after Sunday morning Bible class. A parent asked his young daughter: "What did you learn at class today?" Very innocently and truthfully she replied: "Nothing!" He asked her again: "Why not?" She replied: "I already knew it!" He then asked, in jest: "So what was the point?" Quite seriously---not realizing he was joking with her---she shrugged her shoulders.

Church of Christ members---typically very serious and dedicated---realize the pointlessness to most of the sermons and classes they have to sit and silently endure, so have learned to manufacture another "point" to their gatherings: seeing and briefly speaking with good friends, relatives, and acquaintances.

They've learned to not expect anything of value in their sermons or classes, which they studiously and dutifully "put up with" out of a sense of resigned duty. The only predictable value to the exercise is a short time of fellowship at the beginning or end of the religious ritual.

**Suggested Action Items:**
- In sermons, lectures, and Bible discussions *focus on <u>Jesus</u>* --- yes, everything else in the Bible is interesting and helpful. But for Christians the focus should be on Jesus.
- *Acknowledge that Jesus' <u>actions</u> are critically-important* to inform us today *HOW* we should implement the teachings of Jesus.
- *Discern and emphasize the <u>Radical Principles</u> of Jesus* as powerful mandates flexible enough to control our thoughts, words, and actions today and on into the unpredictable future.
- *Involve people* in sermons, lecture classes, and Bible discussion instead of them just having the "great privilege" of hearing you speak your mind.
- Look to *help people discover the answers for themselves* --- rather than handing them "the" Answer: mostly by patiently asking key thoughtful questions.
- In personal evangelism Bible studies *move people quickly up the "learning-effectiveness curve"* by doing the following: 1) focus on reading one or two key books in the bible (Such as John and Romans); 2) allow the person to read him-or-herself a passage; 3) ask the person what he or she found most interesting (from either a positive or negative standpoint) in that passage; 4) facilitate discussion with that person and anyone else present by asking them further targeted questions stimulating them to struggle with discovering their own valid answers; and 5) repeat with the next passage.

- *Take an interested person with you* and train them in how to do effective visitation, effective personal Bible study, and effective Christian activity. This is the time-honored "apprenticeship" method of effective teaching of skills.
- Then *train them in how to train others.*

23) **Stop preaching that members are failing in evangelism because they are too weak or embarrassed to just "tell people what Jesus has done for you"** --- JESUS SUCCESSFULLY EVANGELIZED WITHIN COORDINATED, COMPLEX CAMPAIGNS COMBINING TOGETHER AND MOBILIZING THE TALENTS OF MANY PEOPLE!

We tend to envision Jesus sitting on top of a mountain giving a sermon to motivate people---forgetting that a lot went on to contact the people, bring the people, and keep them there. It wasn't just climbing up on a mountain to give a sermon and having people flock around you to hear it!

Plus, to interest people today in actively following Jesus' teachings is far more difficult than in Jesus' time. Jesus himself stated that it's almost impossible for a rich man to get into heaven. In our developed, industrialized societies even the "poor" are richer than the Kings of Jesus' times in all the ways that truly matter: 1) access to effective health care, 2) cheap, amazingly-useful technological devices, 3) expert, extended education for their children, 4) career opportunity, and 5) ready access to plentiful food.

Today in our advanced society we are all rich! When your immediate needs are reasonably met, God often becomes a nice option rather than a critical necessity.

Furthermore, the Great Commission of Jesus to "go into the entire world and preach the Gospel to every creature" has largely been accomplished! Who in our society hasn't heard about Jesus, knows the main things about his life, and has *already* made a decision on how to respond to Jesus?

Happily *informing* people of an amazing spiritual thing they've never heard of before---has become difficult *persuasion*! Either they are already a (mostly inherited from birth) member of this or that Christian group, have decided to believe but not be part of a formal religious group, or have decided not to believe at all.

People on hearing "what Jesus has done for you" may be happy for what you've experienced, but feel little relation of those events to their own life. Either they don't perceive a personal need at all; or they've already made their decision for their own life. They might agree it is fine you want to go down to that church there on the corner and spend a lot of time and money there. But your decision for your own life doesn't affect them!

Today it takes a serious, ongoing, well-constructed, well-supported, multi-faceted effective Program to interest people in becoming part of your religious group! So if you are not willing to put out the study, the time, the careful experimentation, and the work to gear up and maintain a serious evangelistic Program at your congregation then *STOP BEATING UP YOUR MEMBERS FOR "FAILING" AT PERSONAL EVANGELISM*!

Not only does "preaching harder" *not* motivate your people to success, it *discourages* them from even trying!

**Possible Action Items:**
- Instead of preaching that people need only "tell other people what Jesus has done for you" *teach people effective tools* for interesting people in active Christianity.
- Instead of vague generalities, *show videos or bring in speakers of how other Christians effectively interest people* in being part of their congregations;
- Encourage people by *illustrating how their particular different talents can contribute* positively to a friendship-evangelism, congregational program.
- *Preach and teach in visitor-friendly ways* --- starting with real problems that people have and using that focus to get-into different Bible teachings. In other

words, give your members the value-added environment that they would be comfortable urging their friends outside the church to attend!
- *Help build and advertise visitor-friendly mechanisms* --- such as small-group, home-based, Bible fellowship groups focused on real-world, pressing problems instead of just advocating the "right" doctrine.

. . . . . . . . . . . . . . . . . . . . . . . . . . . . . . . . . . . . . . . . . . . . . . . . . . .

**24) <u>Stop waiting for "sinners" to come to you</u>** --- JESUS WENT TO WHERE THE SINNERS WERE AT!

First of all, please note that by "sinners" I don't mean people who go to some other church where they supposedly "worship in error." Unfortunately, this has substituted in the tradition of the Church of Christ for people who are not interested in Jesus. Please wish those at other Christian groups the best, and then focus on people who are actually hurting themselves doing bad things to themselves and others!

Now that we know what we're talking about, let's get serious. One of the biggest problems killing evangelistic efforts in Church of Christ congregations is expecting that "sinners" will somehow want to come down to the church building to be preached at on how bad they are! In fact, the very opposite is true.

Couples living together outside of marriage, people who enjoy alcohol or smoking, people who like to party on Saturday night then sleep in on Sunday mornings, people who abuse and misuse others...these are all things that people know the Bible says are "sin"; so they deliberately and consciously have zero desire to go to the churches that they know will condemn them!

And yet Church of Christ preachers will get up and fervently preach to their audiences as if those people were all vile sinners needing to get saved! Presumably these preachers preaching so fervently to the wrong people are somehow expecting the membership to go and corner a bunch of sinners, tie them up, and drag them into the church building to hear the condemnation sermons! Ain't going to happen!

JESUS WENT SO FAR AS TO EVEN GO INTO THE HOUSES OF SINNERS AND EAT DINNER WITH THEM! JESUS LEFT THE SYNAGOGUES AND TEMPLE IN ORDER TO

PREACH OUT IN THE OPEN WHERE ANYONE COULD COME AND HEAR HIM!

Yes, it's true that the street-corner, "on-the-crate" preacher would likely be arrested today by police for disturbing the peace. However, there are places that people who behave in ways the Bible speaks against do congregate. There are appropriate ways to interface into those establishments with Biblical messages.

If all else fails, most of the "sinners" have homes! Here I'm not talking about knocking randomly on doors. I'm talking about changing the emphasis from "preaching the Truth" in a church building to finding good ways to be invited into the homes of interested "non-churched" people---or have them come to our own homes!

Yes, we're back to "friendship-evangelism" identifying people we already have positive connections with, respectfully asking for appointments to visit them in their homes, and having expert teams invite them into already-established, already well-working, visitor-friendly, small-group fellowships or activities. Just accept the fact that non-churched people are *not* going to come on their own to your church building! You have to go to *them*.

Yes, this is complicated, difficult, and even somewhat dangerous. Also, not everyone has the talent to do this. Again, it requires a well-designed, well-supported, program where a number of people with the appropriate talents work together on an ongoing basis.

**Possible Action Items:**
- Occasionally *hold the entire Sunday morning church service in the town's public park or some other public space*: of course getting all necessary permits, constructing a truly visitor-friendly program, offering something of real value that non-churched people

might be interested in (such as a talk by a recognized expert on how the Bible and Jesus would help with some big problem people in the community have), coupled with free food afterwards---extensively advertised and promoted beforehand!
- *Go to existing community groups and forums* --- taking with you expert, value-added information or services that promote Jesus and your congregation while also meeting their particular needs.
- *Provide expert group meetings for overcoming sinful behaviors* --- such as healthy marriage counseling, troubled children management, grief recovery, overcoming drug addiction, tobacco-quitting groups, anger-management therapy, etc. (all tied closely to the Bible, Jesus, and your congregation).
- Have a well-constructed, well-supported, effective *congregational friendship-evangelism program* to respectfully make appointments for expert teams to go into non-churched people's homes.
- When you do have the opportunity to meet sinners where they are at, *teach respectfully and sympathetically by polite questions and helpful information* (no lectures and no sermons).

. . . . . . . . . . . . . . . . . . . . . . . . . . . . . . . . . . . . . . . . . . . . . . . . . . .

**25) Instead of looking to "save" people, look to *help* them in Christ-like ways that *they* will readily agree are helpful** --- JESUS' MESSAGE WAS DELIVERED HAND-IN-GLOVE WITH REAL TANGIBLE HELP WHERE THE PEOPLE WERE SUFFERING THE MOST!

One of the worst strategies of Church of Christ preachers trying to encourage evangelism is to harangue members into seeing people as either "saved" or "damned"! Compounding this is the clear message that anything different from the traditional beliefs and practices done by the Church of Christ is "in error" and thus puts the practitioners thereof in danger of damnation.

This, of course, is phrased as "disobeying God"---defined as not agreeing with the Church of Christ doctrines: expressed as "just read the Bible" on what God wants! This view ignores the fact that many of the Church of Christ doctrines aren't even in the New Testament, but are actually handed-down generational beliefs based on a scattering of verses tied together with debatable assumptions.

But, being told to "just read the Bible" implies that everything is spelled out in detail in the Bible and is exactly what God wants---although many other knowledgeable Christian individuals and groups disagree! In this "black" or "white" world anyone not attending the local Church of Christ congregation is viewed as either damned or in imminent danger of damnation.

Although preachers and church leaders of the Church of Christ are reluctant to admit this viewpoint, the self-imposed isolation and arrogance of their congregations is obvious to outsiders. You deciding that I am "damned" because I don't meet your particular religious standards (no matter how sincerely you believe in those standards), is something that I find neither helpful nor respectful! If you are not respectful of me, then why should I respect (listen to) your viewpoints?

However, there's another way to approach people evangelistically that is very different from viewing them as damned sinners in need of salvation.

JESUS APPROACHED HIS GENERATION AS PEOPLE WHO NEEDED HELP FOR MOVING CLOSER TO GOD. JESUS PROVED HIS SINCERE DESIRE TO HELP PEOPLE BY ACTUALLY DOING IT IN WAYS THAT THEY AGREED WERE HELPFUL: CURING INCURABLE PHYSICAL ILLNESS, FEEDING THEM WHEN THEY WERE HUNGRY, FELLOWSHIPPING WITH THEM WHEN REGULAR RELIGION DISTAINED THEM, SYMPATHETIC TO THEIR PROBLEMS, SPEAKING TO THE MAJOR CONCERNS OF THEIR GENERATION IN TERMS THEY COULD READILY UNDERSTAND, REFUSING TO CONDEMN THEM EVEN WHEN THEY DESERVED SUCH, RESPECTFULLY GOING TO WHERE THEY WERE AT, NOT REQUIRING DIFFICULT RITUALS AS A REQUIREMENT OF THEIR CONVERSION, AND OFFERING THEM PERSONAL FRIENDSHIP.

Viewing people sympathetically as them being honest people struggling against hard problems changes the entire dynamics of "evangelism." Instead of thinking: "how can I cleverly word my arguments and debates to prove to them they should get properly baptized and come be lectured-at in my church building" one now *first* thinks: "How can I help them with their problems in a way that explicitly shows them Jesus?"

The interaction changes from a difficult debate to an offered friendly, helping hand. The task is then to extend that helping hand from me to Jesus to God.

Those that are truly converted to Jesus have no problem at all with baptism or any of the other enabling aspects of formal religion. As to who is "saved" or "damned"---why not let God sort it out?

Preachers often fall back on that poorest motivating factor of all: engendered guilt. The implicit message is: "*YOU* are letting *THEM* go to *HELL!*" Rather than guilt, why not be motivated out of the love of God for His wayward, confused, hurting children? Offer the helping-hand of Jesus! Show them Jesus not just in theory but in action!

Church Leaders, provide the well-constructed, effective Programs where members can contribute the many different talents needed to actually *HELP* people with their problems in a Jesus-centered manner! Yes, this is not simple, easy, or safe! Yes, it is complicated, hard, and even sometimes dangerous!

But motivating by guilt or fear is self-defeating. Motivating with joy and love is self-renewing. Provide good mechanisms that actually work to help people move closer to God!

**Possible Action Items:**
- Based on the existing talents and resources of your congregation, decide on *Jesus-based effective mechanisms to help people* in your community solve one or more of their worst problems (such as specific counseling groups, etc.)
- *See if existing parts of your weekly or monthly church schedule might be re-purposed* to the main goal of helping non-churched people with their problems in your community. (A good example is the traditional monthly "pot-luck" meal for the congregation. The many times I've done this there was no purpose except to sit next to your present friends at the church and share a meal. Why not make this an outreach to the hungry in the community? Search for and invite a specific family, advertise it in general in the local paper for anyone to attend, or ask the group to bring

enough food to then be able to take meals to identified poor people to eat with them in their own homes!)
- *Provide group-targeted small-group Bible study fellowships* --- a common problem in our society is isolation. People are looking for meaningful personal, friendly contacts beyond electronic internet relationships. Build effective home-based small groups for fellowship/Jesus-study for the various age and categories of people in your community.
- *Read a book, bring in experts, or go "bench-mark" successful groups* --- on how to make work the mechanisms you identify as best possibilities for your congregation to implement for offering Jesus-based help to people of your community.
- *Do what you can on a person-to-person basis to offer the helping hand of Jesus,* but realizing that without effective support by the Church Leadership with fundamental improvements to be visitor-friendly you'll have little chance of convincing them to regularly come to church.

. . . . . . . . . . . . . . . . . . . . . . . . . . . . . . . . . . . . . . . . . . . . . . . . . . . . .

26) **Connect effective benevolence to meaningful religious requirements** --- JESUS REQUIRED PEOPLE TO DO THINGS GOOD FOR THEMSELVES IN ORDER TO BECOME HIS DISCIPLES!

Church of Christ benevolence typically does nothing to promote evangelism. It has this unproductive result mainly because of a blind adherence to the Bible concept of "give asking for nothing in return."

Clearly the meaning is to give freely in an unselfish manner. Requiring people who want benevolence from us to do things that are good for *them* is a concept other Christian groups understand and implement.

What sort of things might be required? Well, how about taking some of their time to attend the service! How about sitting down for a few minutes to read and discuss a few key scriptures in the Bible that apply directly to their situation? How about answering questions about their spiritual lives? How about requiring attendance at a future date to the church services? How about bowing their heads for a prayer on their behalf?

Are they not asking us to give to them things of value (money, clothes, food, or shelter)? Why should they not give something of value of theirs in return (time, interest, discussion, attention, or participation) if that thing that will be good for *them*?

If people are coming to us for help then they should expect that we church people will require them to receive not only physical but spiritual help from us as well! If approached properly, this can be an occasion not just for making ourselves feel that we're doing good deeds, but occasionally having real opportunities for effective evangelism.

**Possible Action Items:**
- *Write a Benevolence Policy* --- printed and handed out to anyone seeking benevolence that spells out what we are willing to do under what circumstances; and what they must do (that's good for them) to receive such help. Typically, benevolence in mainline Church of Christ congregations is handled on a case-by-case basis with little or no thought to spiritual requirements.
- *Proactively offer benevolence* --- prepare a proactive benevolence policy (such as an ad in the local paper: "We will help you with__(X)__ if you are willing to do __(Y)__ that's good for you!" This is not just to wait until someone discovers the church and comes begging, but to offer what we are capable of doing proactively to the community, in search of those truly in need who are willing to meet our spiritual, evangelistic requirements! (Of course this would be carefully budgeted so as to not "break the bank" with a flood of applicants.)
- *Offer short scholarships to local schools, short paid internships in Christian activities, and defined, short jobs* --- requiring various spiritual commitments to the local congregation; to both help those in need while bringing in "new blood" to the congregation.
- *Start a contest* --- advertised in the local paper, for best poem/song/short-story/painting etc. on a Bible theme complete with a monetary reward: with the spiritual requirement of presenting such at an appropriate church gathering where the prize is awarded!

. . . . . . . . . . . . . . . . . . . . . . . . . . . . . . . . . . . . . . . . . . . . . . . . . . . . . . .

**27) Tangibly place your own children as your #2 church priority, coming in only behind Jesus** --- JESUS CONDEMNED THOSE THAT INHIBITED CHILDREN FROM COMING TO HIM!

A shameful situation exists in many Church of Christ congregations in which their own children are at the bottom of the congregation's priorities. "Surely," you say, "you must be mistaken!?" No, I'm not.

If you look at the yearly budget of mainline Church of Christ congregations you will see that the "youth program" often gets little or nothing. Indeed, it is typically not even a line-item in the budget at all! If queried on this, the Church Leaders may point to "Bible school supplies" as the youth budget. Sorry, folks---a few "Mickey-Mouse" type simplistic fill-in Bible study booklets *isn't* a youth program!

If you want to know what your top priorities are, just look at how you spend your own money. If you want to know what the true priorities of a congregation are, likewise look at their budget. Our own children in our congregations often come behind paying for a comfortable preacher, a comfortable building, utilities, and a small evangelism effort half the world away. Of course, after paying for all those things there's typically nothing left. So that's what the youth gets...nothing! And for nothing, the result that you get is...nothing.

Here is my challenge to all mainline Church of Christ congregations: set aside the first ten percent of all contributions into a protected "youth fund." Note I am not asking for 90% or 50% but just the first dollar out of each ten. 90% is still left to pay for all the lesser-priority "house-keeping" things. (If at the end of the month you can't pay the water bill, take up a special collection. But announcing and continuing to promote your "putting first things first" budget will likely result in an increased collection anyway.)

Put together an appropriate "youth committee" composed of parents, teachers, other interested people, and key young people. Have them come up with one excellent Christian youth activity per quarter (not just going to an amusement park) of real impact for their fellowship, meaningful service, and spiritual growth. Approve the activities that you feel are appropriate and pay for all costs of everyone involved out of the fund.

Also, allow the youth to bring friends with them on the grand activities, paying all costs for them as well (as many as the funds will allow). Since youth have no money of their own and haven't yet made up their minds about Jesus they are the one identifiable group left in developed countries susceptible to overt, excellent evangelism (who are neither rich, fully informed on Jesus, nor decided).

Improve your services, classes, and small-group meetings to be "youth friendly" and you might have a shot at not only keeping your own children but recruiting those of other parents as well!

Why is this not already routinely done? Well, first of all parents have this idea that children need to learn to suffer the same as parents: i.e. to learn to sit quietly during long, boring sermons and lectures which offer nothing much beyond first-principle doctrines. I guess this *is* a good lesson in *endurance*, but a *negative* lesson in church offering anything of real value to meeting their valid, perceived needs.

Secondly, parents/teachers/key-young-people have great ideas as to how to have meaningful fellowship, service, and spiritual growth projects...but all the best ones cost money! They know not to go to the church leadership for money because there's never any money beyond just barely paying for the existing top priorities. They know that the children are the last priority, for which even if the leadership wanted to fund some excellent activities there's no money left!

And third, the church leadership and parents have the mistaken idea that the best thing to keep their children in the faith is to indoctrinate them properly in "Bible Classes." Somehow to learn all the Old Testament stories, memorize verses, recite the books of the Bible, and agree to the Church of Christ doctrines is supposed to convert their children to Jesus. Wrong.

When "church" is synonymous with "school" then the joy is immediately drained away. Just as the kids can't wait to graduate from school into the real world, they are happy to quit the church for something more meaningful---either to live their own life or join a religious group better resembling the Jesus they read about in the Bible.

The children get the unspoken message. Many of the kids once having reached the "age of accountability" do reluctantly agree to be baptized to get the adults off their backs, but often not out of lasting conviction. As soon as they are out on their own, most opt to leave: to quit entirely or go to some other religious group where it's joyful, interesting, inspirational, helpful, and productive.

They choose to go to a place where Christianity is more than just conforming to prevailing doctrines. They choose to go to places where children are in fact put as the #2 (not last) priority. They choose to go to places where the #1 priority is actually "walking in the footsteps of Jesus."

Instead of lecturing kids on Christian doctrine, why not lead them to actually walk in the footsteps of Jesus?

**Possible Action Items:**
- *Set aside the first 10% of each contribution* into a protected Youth Fund.
- Appoint a *Youth Activity Committee* composed of parents, teachers, other interested adults, and key young-people.
- Have the Youth Activity Committee identify possible *excellent quarterly activities* where the young people (in related age groups) can have extraordinary opportunities for Christian service, fellowship, and spiritual growth.
- *Leadership approves and funds* appropriate, big activities.
- The *services and classes of the church are improved* to be youth-friendly (while still hitting on the appropriate teachings of the Bible).
- Slots are opened up for your children to *invite a certain number of friends* to the big activities, paid for entirely by the Youth Fund.
- THE 10% FUND IS <u>NOT</u> DISSIPATED BY SPENDING IT TO HIRE A "YOUTH MINISTER" to bore them with yet more lectures and trivial, Mickey-Mouse-type activities--- but spent entirely and directly on the young people themselves: as spent and orchestrated by themselves and their adult advocates.

------------------------------------------------

## Chapter Five:

# CHURCH MANAGEMENT

28) **Stop being proud of being amateurs** --- JESUS APPROACHED HIS CAMPAIGNS AND EVENTS AS A WELL-PREPARED, STATE-OF-THE-ART, MASTER TEACHER!

First of all, those good-hearted men who voluntarily take upon themselves all the headaches and responsibilities of church leadership, for no pay as appointed Elders and Deacons, are to be thanked. They uniformly take their duties very seriously and do their best to guide their congregations in Godly ways. I say: "Thank you for your unselfish service! This is very commendable that you are willing to take on these heavy responsibilities."

Likewise, those highly-talented men who are willing to take on the many duties of being church ministers, typically for low pay, are also to be commended. To them I also offer a sincere: "Thank you!" Having said that, please *stop* being *proud* of being *amateurs*!

Mainline Church of Christ appointed Church Leaders (Elders, Deacons, and Ministers) typically have an "ah shucks" attitude that they're just local members themselves, largely do the work themselves as regular members, and reject the "trappings of power" that other Christian groups sometimes adopt. All of that is admirable except that it biases people against rising to the occasion of rejecting Tradition if it conflicts with Jesus.

Anything "new" or "different" is often automatically rejected as "wrong"---whether or not it might help better-inspiring youth, appeal to visitors, or retain members. "What we've got is good enough!" may or may not be true, depending upon the objective. In fact, innovations are often jeered at for the very fact that they are intended to interest young people and visitors!

This is not a professional attitude! This is being proud of being amateurs, who look not to principle but to methodology regardless of results!

Being proud of being amateurs stems from five main beliefs: 1) to know and preach only Jesus; 2) that the New Testament church was already given "all things necessary for life and godliness"; 3) that individual congregations have to remain self-sufficient and autonomous; 4) that the job of church leaders is to "defend and feed the flock"; 5) that they have absolute church power forever; and 6) ministerial authority is subservient to the Elders.

Knowing and preaching only Jesus isn't necessarily bad if that were true. However, like many other small Christian denominations, the Church of Christ knows and preaches the traditional beliefs and practices handed down by previous generations *instead* of going back *de novo* to Jesus!

As to having been given "all things necessary for life and godliness" this is absolutely true in regards to Principles. But the Application thereto in all situations, all societies, and all circumstances is *NOT* given to us! The Principle may be clear, but its application can be extremely confusing---for which we may need to study, test, and struggle!

The Bible is often viewed as a blueprint for Christ's Church. It is not. It is a book of Questions leaving you to struggle to find the Answers for your particular time and society. Jesus came to give us Radical Principles for transforming our hearts and lives---not point-by-point instructions for doing "proper" rituals!

The New Testament simply *DOES NOT STATE HOW TO "DO" CHURCH*! Church of Christ congregations fall back on a "pattern" they see in the Bible which *isn't* there! The "pattern" is found in traditional beliefs and practices for which a scattering of isolated verses is stitched together with inserted assumptions.

Thus Principles are indeed present in the New Testament while the Application is mostly missing! This, however, is too difficult for most people to struggle with---opting instead for resolving it all down to set doctrines, exact rituals, settled ceremonies, and exclusionary practices: all "sanctified" by Tradition!

Elevating Tradition above the Principles of Jesus greatly handicaps Church of Christ leadership in rising above the status of amateurs. The Church of Christ leadership is further crippled by the belief (also not found in the New Testament) that individual congregations must not have any hierarchy above them.

Other Christian groups have no problem with an overall management system or hierarchy above the local congregation. What this allows them to do is to have the resources to establish clear training, certification, and knowledge systems.

The one requirement to be a preacher for a Church of Christ congregation is to be a male willing to take the meager pay offered. There exist a few tiny Church of Christ "preacher schools" that focus almost entirely on teaching how to defend the traditional Church of Christ doctrines. Thus you get preachers who learn ministry work "by the seat of their pants," with no formal training or certification---who think that the best preaching of all is to make an intellectual defense of a doctrinal position: and who make fun of other types of preaching as merely superficially "motivational."

There also exist a few theological programs at accredited Church of Christ-associated colleges. My understanding of these programs is that they focus mainly on theological aspects, not the gritty techniques of successful church management or ministry.

As to the key, critical leadership positions of Elders and Deacons, to my knowledge there exists no formal training programs at all to give them the skills and knowledge to successfully manage a local congregation. Once again, these good-hearted people taking on heavy management duties learn "by the seat of their pants."

Thus the leadership of the local Church of Christ congregation has little or no idea how to effectively manage a volunteer, nonprofit organization. Lacking the skills to do the job, they fall back on the much-easier *AIM* of maintaining Tradition: encapsulated by my statement of "Defend the Truth!"

Maintaining the "status quo"---whether or not it accomplishes desired objectives---is easy. Just do everything the same as you've always done, allowing nothing different! Responding intelligently to actual valid spiritual needs of your particular mix of people in your congregation and in your community is a difficult, complicated, and delicate task! Perhaps your traditional beliefs and practices will work fine. Likely they won't.

In that case the amateur manager facing a novel situation has no idea what to do! The professional manager knows how to learn to do better! The professional manager is aware and willing to contemplate a whole variety of methods and techniques for best-accomplishing the job at hand. The professional manager knows how volunteer organizations differ from businesses where most people are hired, paid, and fired! The professional nonprofit manager knows how to effectively interest, motivate, and help volunteers use their talents together.

Other Christian groups are able to train, equip, and support the leadership at their local congregations. Church of Christ congregations have no such support structure to fall back on when things don't work or unexpected problems arise.

Furthermore, the Elders and Deacons are not even appointed by the local Church of Christ congregation on the basis of their fitness to do the job. These men are selected on two main criteria: 1) not having been divorced (successful marriage), and 2) having more than one child who were at some point in the past baptized (believing children). There are other general requirements listed in the New Testament for Christian congregations appointing leadership, but the two I stated are the main *excluders*.

Since in our present society where casual divorce is common (even among Church of Christ members, though Jesus strictly forbade the practice), birth control is easy to obtain (thus having no children or only one child is common), plus children often fall away and never get baptized at all---men with a successful marriage and more than one believing children are quite rare!

So it's typical to find in the rare man who has this minimally-required qualification to be an Elder or Deacon...a person that has absolutely no idea, no skill, and zero training for successfully managing a volunteer, nonprofit organization! And since there is no supporting hierarchy, that person is almost totally isolated with nothing to fall back on.

Plus, to compound the mounting negatives, members of the congregation feel compelled to "submit to authority" such that the only responses possible to bad decisions by the managers are to withdraw one's talents, cut one's donation, or leave the congregation entirely!

Even worse, Elders and Deacons do not have term limits. They are appointed for life. For them, the only recourse to deteriorating conditions is to ignominiously and shamefully quit. When things "go bad" in congregations, it's common for the Leadership to quit the church entirely or move to some other congregation within driving distance. So it's "all or nothing" where the leadership often isn't even aware of their own ignorance in how to successfully manage a volunteer organization.

And where they do understand that they, indeed, are amateurs, they turn that into a "virtue" by being proud of it! In their own eyes they're not "business people" using "business techniques" but humble serving brothers! But JESUS WAS NOT AN AMATEUR. JESUS WAS A MASTER TEACHER WHO KNEW HOW TO BEST MOTIVATE, ORGANIZE, AND DIRECT PEOPLE.

That Jesus was able to rise to the position of threatening the entire Jewish establishment of his time showed his skill and professionalism. *The Church of Christ leadership today should strive to be like Jesus*: taking upon their selves the responsibility to study, train, and continually learn better how to successfully manage a volunteer organization.

Finally, the lines of authority are confused and mangled between the paid minister and the Eldership. Other Christian groups often deliberately cede operational authority to a trained and certified Minister or Priest (functioning in essence as a CEO, "chief executive officer" or COO, "Chief Operating Officer"). The appointed local leadership then operates as a Board of Directors who can dismiss or request dismissal of the Minister or Priest should they do bad things. But the day-to-day authority is largely delegated to the trained Minister.

In Church of Christ congregations the local Eldership with little or no training in nonprofit management insists of taking operational authority as well as oversight authority. So even when the rare minister is hired who does have skill in managing nonprofits, that person is severely handicapped by the local amateur leadership. Often the response to ministers trying to implement improvements for retaining youth, interesting visitors, and inspiring members is to be fired.

**Possible Action Items:**
- Go to Amazon.com and type into the search window: "volunteer organizations" or "managing nonprofit organizations" or "leading churches" and you will *find a number of excellent books* you can order and have in your hands within a few days by experts giving you key techniques and methods for professional church management.
- Select a few up-to-date books that look particularly useful and interesting---and *read them*!
- Schedule regular not-rushed, relaxed times when you as leaders of your congregation can *discuss the book* you've all just read.
- Go to YouTube.com and type into the search window similar terms as you did at Amazon.com. *View short, free videos* of people talking and presenting excellent techniques and information on successfully managing volunteer organizations.
- And/or *bring in guest speakers* who are expert in managing volunteer organizations such as yours to present and discuss with you various aspects thereof.
- *Bring in professional consultants* to help with good management options you'd like to implement or are having trouble with in your local congregation: especially when facing new problems or opportunities!
- *Be humble, admitting your shortcomings---but proud of learning* ever-better how to successfully manage a nonprofit, volunteer organization.
- *Change your AIM* from "Defend the Truth" to "*Do* the Truth."

. . . . . . . . . . . . . . . . . . . . . . . . . . . . . . . . . . . . . . . . . . . . . . . . . . . . . .

29) **Stop insulting the intelligence and talents of your people** --- JESUS SELECTED HIGHLY TALENTED PEOPLE, LED THEM BY EXAMPLE, AND CHALLENGED THEM TO RISE TO THEIR FULL POTENTIAL!

Church of Christ congregations offer trivial involvement (word a short prayer, help pass out communion trays, read a short scripture) to a few men, rather than recognizing and helping *all* members to use their talents *together* implementing the Radical Principles of Jesus.

Church of Christ congregations typically focus on defending their traditional Doctrines---particularly first-principle "milk"---rather than offering value-added information and platforms for how to better-implement the Radical Principles of Jesus.

Church of Christ Bible classes typically ignore the spiritual maturity of their audience and instead present rote-explanations of Bible books to people that have already gone through the same material in the same way numerous times. Rituals take the place of productive action. Procedure takes the place of Purpose.

Instead of engaging children in meaningful discussion of the Radical Jesus or involving them in implementing Jesus' Principles, the kids are subjected to "Mickey-Mouse" type workbooks often insisting on going through the entire Bible regardless of the applicability to present-day problems. In striving to be the "intellectuals" of the Christian world, Church of Christ congregations often, incongruously, treat their adults like children.

Church of Christ congregations delegate leadership to Elders that rarely consult their people on spiritual decisions. Yet spiritual deliberation of Elderships is typically minimal or absent: almost never asking if what the congregation does meets desired objectives.

Church of Christ congregations often have monthly "Men's Business Meetings" (not found in the New Testament) to supposedly engage men (not the women) who are not a part of the official leadership into the work of the church. Even though it is labeled as "business" the assumption is that this is a leadership function satisfying the need to provide church leadership. Unfortunately, little or nothing of spiritual consequence is discussed or achieved in these brief monthly meetings.

Church of Christ congregations rarely if ever ask for or provide a workable mechanism to receive feedback from their members, visitors, or young people. The attitude is that "What we're doing is perfect and if you don't like it, too bad!" If feedback is nonetheless offered it's usually seen as a personal insult, hurtful criticism, or as blatant selfishness ("They just want things their way!")---or as actual heresy (seeking to harm the congregation by evilly changing things)!

In Church of Christ congregations there is no framework for identifying, supporting, and linking the talents of the membership. Noteworthy initiatives are often individually-started efforts which are just as likely to be demonized and stopped by the leadership as supported.

A "good" member is a person who keeps his or her mouth shut, attends the required meetings, and regularly donates a generous amount of money.

Children are expected to keep their mouths shut, learn to sit silently during adult-level preaching and lectures, and get baptized once they are teenagers. Nothing more is expected.

Members are expected to be happy to sing the same set of songs over and over, hear the same mumbled prayers over and over, gladly listen to sermons focused mainly on defending accepted doctrines, and be happy to have church time filled with repetitive Bible study rather than Bible application.

Women are expected to keep their mouths shut, leave all leadership to the men, and stay in their place (subservient to the men). Efforts by women to self-organize and do good things beyond caring for young children are likely to be denied support by the leadership, suppressed, or actively shutdown.

Official doctrine denies any established science that seems to conflict with traditional beliefs, no matter how tenuous the Bible reasoning or how verified the science. Preachers with a good grasp of the compelling teachings of Jesus undermine the validity of their own words when they insist that the Bible is a science book when it is not.

The Bible is a spiritual book, not a science book. All of the books of the Bible, including the book of Genesis, teach spiritual messages, not science! When preachers grasp at a few scattered verses that supposedly show science (when they clearly do not) to try and prove "where the Bible refers to science it is true" they undermine the spiritual message of Jesus.

This is most obvious when preachers insist that the creation accounts in Genesis must be taken completely literally (although in other major parts of the Bible such as Revelation, somehow it's ok to understand them to be symbolic language---when no such allowance is indicated, and they also are presented in a completely "literal" fashion!).

As to the Creation of the world, there is a clear Christian Account that Church of Christ preachers and teachers ignore: in the first chapter of the Gospel of John. For Christians, as stated there in the New Testament, the creation of the world is a very simple, profound, spiritual message: "IN THE BEGINNING WAS THE WORD. THE WORD WAS WITH GOD

AND WAS GOD. HE WAS WITH GOD IN THE BEGINNING. THROUGH HIM ALL THINGS WERE MADE. WITHOUT HIM NOTHING WAS MADE THAT HAS BEEN MADE. IN HIM WAS LIFE. THAT LIFE WAS THE LIGHT OF MEN. THE LIGHT SINES IN THE DARKNESS, BUT THE DARKNESS HAS NOT UNDERSTOOD IT. THE WORD BECAME FLESH AND DWELLED AMONG US. WE HAVE SEEN HIS GLORY, FULL OF GRACE AND TRUTH."

This is the "Creation Story" that Church of Christ preachers should preach! When preachers obsess on how and when the universe, the earth, and life were created by God---they should focus entirely on talking about Jesus! Christians have their own, powerful Creation Story! It clearly is *not* giving science details (as to exactly what physical, biological, and mathematical mechanisms were in play) on how God caused the universe, the world, and life to develop---and neither does the Old Testament account! Symbolic language (understandable by anyone of any time-period regardless of their knowledge or grasp of science) is used to teach deep, profound spiritual realities!

Today, with our vast wealth of knowledge of the physical, biological, and mathematical mechanisms of God's nature, insisting on trying to make the Bible into a science text book when it clearly isn't causes people to think thusly: "If this preacher who sounds so convincing can be so wrong on clear science matters, how can I believe anything else he's telling me?"

This disconnect is made even worse by preachers insisting in their apologetic arguments that they understand the key things about science (such as in regards to biology, geology, physics, anthropology, evolution, or global weather mechanisms) when the very words they use reveal abysmal ignorance on that particular science subject!

And in defense of other traditional doctrines (other than science-related), visitors often hear verses in the Bible clearly twisted from their obvious meanings, other passages being ignored, and assumptions inserted as if they were explicitly written in the New Testament when they are not.

Although the established membership tolerates this traditional "apologetic" reasoning, they do not ignore the insult to their own intelligence. This undermines the compelling spiritual power and validity of Jesus' teachings. Visitors and maturing children are less tolerant. They see a group that's blindly stuck in its own traditions, who fails to put "first-things-first" (making low priorities primary while ignoring top priorities), who offers little of real value for meeting valid personal spiritual and physical needs, where the membership is passively or actively suppressed (particularly women), and where Jesus is an afterthought not the focus.

**Possible Action Items:**
- *Seek helpful feedback* --- by studying how to put in place effective feedback programs, regularly soliciting such, and seriously considering whether the existing efforts are meeting clearly-articulated goals and objectives.
- *Inventory the talents and skills of all your members* --- finding good computer programs to collect the information and access it when needed.
- *Find ways to involve all the membership* in ongoing congregational application of Jesus' teachings: *COMBINING NEEDED TALENTS TO ACHIEVE CLEAR GOALS!*
- *Teach what is truly needed* by the students in the class, which they will agree was useful for them--- *NOT JUST WHAT YOU DECIDE THEY NEED!*
- *First and above all teach children about Jesus* --- if time allows, refer to supporting things in the Bible. If not, drop the other things. Before all else, convert them to Jesus, not just in theory but in practice.

- *Teach by focused, facilitated, meaningful discussion ---* only falling back to short lectures if the material is new to the members of the class.
- *Recognize that in living the Christian Life the members of your class are experts* --- not needing you to lecture them on things they know as well or better than you!
- *Approach evangelism offering meaningful help rather than arrogant condemnation* --- demonstrating the validity of Jesus' teachings by putting them into action.
- *Involve all your people in the process of leadership* --- recognizing that wise delegation of authority is central to what Jesus wanted his disciples to accomplish.
- *Recognize when your membership is spiritually mature* --- upgrading your presentations, lectures, and sermons above the level of first principles.
- *Give equal weight to the "spirit" as to the "understanding"* --- recognizing that joyless intellect has no value.
- *Stick to the spiritual teachings of the Bible* and leave science to the scientists.

. . . . . . . . . . . . . . . . . . . . . . . . . . . . . . . . . . . . . . . . . . . . . . . . . . . .

30) **<u>Stop suppressing women. Instead, encourage and fully support their many talents</u>** --- JESUS DID EVERYTHING HE COULD WITHIN AND BEYOND THE CONSTRAINTS OF HIS SOCIETY AND RELIGION TO PROTECT, PROMOTE, AND EMPOWER WOMEN!

Ok, men. Here's the "bottom line." If you want to save your congregation it's the *women* who are going to do it. Otherwise, you are doomed. But you can be part of the solution, rarely by your own direct efforts but by being in support of your women's work.

Church of Christ congregations take seriously the New Testament teachings about the "role of women": 1) women are not to "usurp" male authority, and 2) women are to "keep silent" at church (even if they have a question about something, to go home to "ask it to their husbands" rather than opening their mouths at church).

One might admire this religious practice deemed extreme by many Christian groups today, as a principled adherence to clear New Testament verses...*if* Church of Christ congregations were not routinely already *violating* it!

In the past, some Christian groups only allowed the women to gather in the back of the room to only observe services since another clear verse in the New Testament states that religious singing is where the members "speak to each other" in psalms and hymns and spiritual songs! Thus when women vocally sing (during this big part of Church of Christ services), according to the Bible they are breaking the prohibition against them speaking!

Furthermore, in mainline Church of Christ congregations women speak and ask questions freely, at church, during Bible classes. Some of the splinter Church of Christ congregations prohibit having Bible classes at their church buildings, partly because women would be allowed to speak there as they do in mainline Church of Christ congregations!

Thus the doctrine against women speaking at church is revealed not so much as a principled position but as a traditional belief handed down from previous generations where the suppression of women was condoned by society in general (only recently in the history of the world were women even allowed to vote in political elections).

As to the Bible principle of women not usurping male authority, that's a clearly based on a decision by the males as to how they decide to *exert* authority. In mainline Church of Christ congregations, past generations decided that it was ok for women to teach children, including male children (as long as they hadn't gotten baptized yet), in Bible classes. Once again, this figures into the prohibition against having church Bible classes in splinter Church of Christ congregations---a clear delegation of authority from the males, allowing women to hold leadership positions over males in some situations!

Other Christian groups have decided that the prohibitions in the New Testament against women in the church were largely societal-based rather than evidence that God, somehow, hates women! These other Christian groups put more emphasis in the clear Bible teaching from Paul that in Christ "there is no slave or slave owner, no Jews or Gentiles, *no male or female*---but *all* are *one* in Jesus!" This is a great Radical Principle based on the teachings of Jesus.

JESUS TOOK EVERY OPPORTUNITY TO SUPPORT AND ELEVATE THE STATUS OF WOMEN, SLAVES, AND THE REJECTED. These were staggeringly-radical Principles for his time and age!

Paul, however, in trying to get the Christian church going, was realistic. He clearly stated his willingness to "become all things to all people in order to win some to Jesus." He even overtly allowed people to keep wrong doctrines in order to not drive them away from Jesus (as in the case of not challenging the wrong doctrine that meat purchased that had been sacrificed to idols was not to be eaten). And in the case of the societal norm of women being the property of males, in order to not doom the nascent Christian church to oblivion, he also compromised the Ideals of Jesus: falling back to the "acceptable" doctrine that dominating male husbands should simply be "good" husbands.

A similar thing occurred with the societal-sanctioned fact of slavery. Instead of dooming the nascent Christian church to instant oblivion by forbidding slavery manifestation in the church (where, according to Paul's own words, all in the church ideally should have been equal whether or not they were women, slaves, or suppressed minorities), he fell back upon the doctrine of just admonishing slave owners to be "good" masters.

In our modern western, industrialized societies we've finally caught up with the Ideals of Jesus and Paul: where slavery is abolished, women are treated as equally-talented people instead of the property of males, and minorities are respected instead of shunned.

The second-class Christian citizenship of "Gentiles" became a non-issue when the Jewish Christian leadership based in Jerusalem was mostly destroyed in the sacking of Jerusalem by the Romans in the first century. By default, most of the Christian church from that point on was composed of the Gentiles championed by Paul.

Historically in the United States, during the bloody Civil War over the fact of slavery, many Christian churches fervently opposed emancipation because of the New Testament verses that clearly endorse the practice of slavery! Today would any Church of Christ member argue that we should return to the odious, ungodly practice of one person owning another as property? And yet this is a clear New Testament allowance for the New Testament church that simply acknowledged the prevailing reality of their society.

The validity of slavery was taught in the New Testament with the same insistence and spiritual-correlates as was the domination of men over women. Therefore, why keep this un-Christ-like practice of suppressing women? If it's ok to stop slavery in the church then why is not also ok to stop suppressing women?

Indeed, in many other Protestant denominations other than the Church of Christ, the men consciously and deliberately ask the women in their group to "use all their talents doing everything." Since mainline Church of Christ groups already go part of the way (delegating to the women some teaching authority and active Bible class participation), why not go all the rest of the way?

The male leadership of a congregation could, if they wished, live up to Paul's teaching of equality in the church not just theoretically (deeming each other spiritually-equal in God's sight while in actuality keeping women as second-class members) but in truth. Not only would this glaring conflict with Christian rhetoric be removed---which strongly informs the rejection of the Church of Christ by young girls, many of the women, visitors, and sliding-out-the-back-door members---but it would affirm the teachings and example of Jesus on this subject.

However, if this traditional belief is too engrained as one of the "self-identity" church doctrines (like prohibiting musical instruments, only one form of baptism acceptable, autonomous congregations, non-fellowship of any differing religious group, or putting Bible study over Bible application) then there exist potentially-viable ways that mainline Church of Christ congregations could still go a long ways toward lifting the suppression of women and better tapping-into their power to save the church.

Men, let's get real. Jesus clearly stated the criteria necessary at the Day of Judgment by which God would allow people to enter heaven. It was *NOT* who made the decisions at church. It was *NOT* who delivered the best sermons or lectures. It was *NOT* who took care of the "business" of running a local congregation. It was those who "fed the hungry, clothed the naked, gave drink to the thirsty, took in the homeless, cared for the sick, and supported those in prison."

Is this what men do? Sure, there's a rare male who is good at those things. Most aren't. Indeed, the "business" of the church at the monthly "men's business meeting" in mainline Church of Christ congregations rarely even mentions any of those things. And yet those are the things that *WILL DETERMINE IF YOUR CONGREGATION GETS INTO HEAVEN*!

Again I ask: "Who does those things?" Answer: "By far, it is the women!" Even the most ardent male leaders of mainline Church of Christ congregations will agree there is "Women's Work" that the females even in the restrictive New Testament times were tasked with doing.

Why not fully appreciate and support the work of the women? Mainline Church of Christ congregations are so against delegating any "leadership" duties to women that they in truth *SUPPRESS* women even in the work that the New Testament confers upon them! *Stop* it, men! If you can not bring yourselves to elevate women to the Ideal of Paul and Jesus...then at least stop suppressing their New Testament-endorsed work!

For more-enlightened leadership, instead of striving to be the "New Testament Church" with all its many failings, why not *BE BETTER THAN* the "New Testament" church---by

*MOVING CLOSER TO THE IDEALS OF JESUS?* But if you can't do this, then at least stop kicking your women down!

Not only might you save yourselves on the Day of Judgment (by having supported those who are doing the critical activities for entering heaven, thus being at least an indirect part of that required behavior) but also save your congregation from dying.

Do you want to revitalize your congregation, connect it to your community, and inspire your young people? Then focus on fully and truthfully encouraging, supporting, and empowering your women!

**Possible Action Items:**
- Humbly *recognize that suppressing your women cripples your congregation* --- doing so publicly and officially. Make an official, public announcement that women are the heart of your congregation, who are henceforth going to be given the recognition and support that they deserve.
- At the monthly "men's business meeting" (an activity not found or authorized in the Bible) instead of leaving your wives at home, bring them for their separate *"Women's Work Meeting"* (plus any other ladies or girls that want to attend). As this is often done right before Sunday evening service, the men typically need to then dash home to "get their wives." Thus bringing them along at the first for their own meeting, to coordinate their own work together, fits in very well. This would allow the females of the congregation to self-organize, synergize, and come up with excellent plans to do the main ongoing work of the church...while the men with good conscience can continue to obsess on fixing leaks in the church building's roof.
- The *male leadership then reviews and approves* any suggested plans and activities of the ladies coming

from their monthly coordination meeting. Thus there is absolutely no "usurping of authority."
- Put into the budget a *line-item for "women's work"* separate from the other categories. Just as with the youth of the congregation, wishful thinking is trumped by deliberate budgeting of real dollars. When the women are given a budget, amazing things become possible!
- *Delegate specific authority to the women* --- for instance, benevolence. We men typically handle benevolence with a super-critical, stingy eye. We look for the deadbeat and the scammer rather than for people in real trouble. Women tend to have greater empathy and capability at expressing the love of Jesus. At the same time, women are very good managers of money. Benevolence and other Christ-like tasks could easily be "off-loaded" to the women by official delegation---allowing them oversight responsibility as well as operational---freeing men to have more time to trim overgrown trees on the church property and do other similar muscular, low-priority tasks.
- *Ask the ladies to use all their talents doing everything* --- Yes, this would be very difficult for most tradition-driven mainline Church of Christ congregations to do. But it is feasible. Other Christian groups do this. The "Usurping Authority" issue is obviated because the men are asking the women to do this! Recognizing that the mainline Church of Christ congregations already are violating the "women keep silent" New Testament rule helps as well in making this big step. Fully empowering the female membership would "uncripple" mainline men-lead Church of Christ congregations as surely as Jesus lifted up the man who'd not walked from birth.

. . . . . . . . . . . . . . . . . . . . . . . . . . . . . . . . . . . . . . . . . . . . . . . . . .

31) **<u>Stop being terrified of the word "Program"</u>** --- JESUS' EVANGELISM EFFORTS WERE WITHIN CAREFULLY-CALIBRATED CAMPAIGNS!

In Church of Christ congregations, "program" has virtually been shortened into a "four-letter," filthy word. It's not clear why this is so.

Possibilities are: 1) the mistaken belief that congregations cannot cooperate amongst themselves; 2) prior failures in trying to sustain ongoing campaigns involving more than two or three people; 3) a general lack of skill or knowledge of how to effectively construct and manage a program; 4) an undefined fear of anything different from the status quo rituals; 5) thinking that their efforts should be mostly spent on "teaching" the Bible; 6) simply having little time to do other than the four ritualistic meetings per week; or 7) thinking that Christian action is mostly an individual responsibility, not the congregation as a whole.

*Whatever the cause, Church of Christ congregations are notorious for having little or no ongoing efforts that significantly impact their communities!* However, other Christian groups in their very same communities are able to do such!

This should be of grave concern to the leadership of the Church of Christ congregations. If their neighboring religious groups are able to visibly extend Christian values into their communities, why cannot the supposed "true" church, the Church of Christ?

If pressed, most Church of Christ congregations will grudgingly admit that they could do better. If further pressed on how or when this will happen, there's no answer.

Church of Christ congregations are extremely reluctant to admit failure. This would be an admission that their doctrinal framework, upon which their efforts rest, is not perfect.

However, if put into different terms---as does this book of mine---even the most conservative leader might be willing to recognize failure as: 1) lack of desired results; and 2) our human condition of never being able to fully live up to Jesus.

First of all, let us all agree that having an ongoing effective program where a number of people contribute their different programs over a protracted period is difficult! Yes, it is hard! Yes, it may even be somewhat dangerous! It may fail! It may require learning new management skills! It may necessitate spending money! It may necessitate spending a lot of one's valuable time! But it might also do the following: 1) energize interested members; 2) serve as a platform where they can exercise and grow their talents on behalf of the congregation; and 3) produce desired results that otherwise would not occur!

So even though reaching a desired goal may be complicated, hard, and a bit dangerous---don't automatically reject trying just because you'd need to construct and maintain a viable "program"!

**Possible Action Items:**
- *Realistically evaluate everything* you do across the congregation as to how well the efforts meet desired, defined goals.
- Where critically-important goals are not being achieved, *ask "Why not?"*
- Without regard to past failures or existing resources, *ask what it would take* to have a shot at achieving or better-meeting those Goals.
- Appoint one or more *small research committees* of people with a strong interest and necessary talents in that area to RESEARCH AND PRESENT SEVERAL CAREFULLY-CONSIDERED OPTIONS FOR MEETING THE CRITICAL GOAL, COMPLETE WITH BOTH THE POSSIBLE DRAWBACKS AND POTEN-

*TIAL POSITIVES OF EACH OPTION* (elevating the discussion of off-the-cuff feelings of people mostly not expert in that particular area, to well-informed people backing up possibilities with real data).
- In one or a few areas where good options are identified, *ask the expert committees to submit detailed plans* on how to accomplish approved programs.
- *Do a small test-run* ("Pilot") of the desired program. *Evaluate* the results. *Improve* the structure. *Test* again. When things are working well, *roll it out* to the entire congregation with strong explanation, promotion, and *ongoing support*.

. . . . . . . . . . . . . . . . . . . . . . . . . . . . . . . . . . . . . . . . . . . . . . . . . . . . . . . . . .

32) **Learn and institute Godly Quality Management** --- JESUS EXHIBITED ALL THE EXCELLENT TOOLS AND TECHNIQUES OF A GODLY QUALITY MANAGER.

As mentioned in prior points, Church of Christ appointed leadership typically appear to be amateurs or incompetents at well-managing a nonprofit volunteer organization.

The first thing needed to reverse this perception is *humility*. These good-hearted, hard-working, dedicated male Christians need to admit to themselves and others that they lack the knowledge and skills to do the best job.

Nobody likes criticism or to accept fault. When confronted with lack of success, many will just quit. JESUS DID NOT QUIT! Even when He met the Ultimate Defeat of being rejected by his own religious leadership, abandoned by most of his closest followers, and condemned to death---Jesus did not give up his commission from God. Instead, HE GREW BEYOND FAILURE INTO ACHIEVING THE GREATEST VICTORY OF ALL!

Being a Minister, an Elder, or a Deacon in the Church of Christ is difficult, demanding, and confusing. It's easy to just give up and let someone else do it. At times, that response may be appropriate, especially if one simply lacks the talent of management. However, the nobler course is to hitch up one's pants, roll up one's sleeves, and forge ahead striving to do and be even better than one is already!

Fortunately, there are extensive resources readily available, for free or for trivial costs, to learn to be and do better as an effective manager of a nonprofit volunteer organization! Yes, most of these are not explicit instruction from the Bible (though they certainly are implied by and reside in the Examples and Principles of the Bible).

For those people who think that every answer is spelled-out in the Bible, though, Godly Wise Management is probably beyond them---and they should seriously consider moving aside for others willing to accept useful detailed information no matter where it comes from.

Also, it's been my experience that Church of Christ leadership rarely reads anything outside of the Bible. But a reluctance to read something that's seen as "work" isn't at all unique to the Church of Christ. "Study" is another of those words that many managers in whatever organization turn into a "four-letter" curse!

After having survived whatever certification they've had to undergo in the past, "study" is seen as being in their past, not in their present! They've already learned how to be managers! Why do they have to keep studying? In fact, the very suggestion that they might need to learn something else is often seen as a reflection on their skills! "How dare you question me!??" is a common attitude if not statement.

"I don't learn, *I* teach!" is another common attitude of many preachers and Bible teachers. But the "proof is in the pudding"! If the pudding is sour---causing guests to gag and retreat, children to cry, and your family to hold their noses as they painfully gulp down the minimally-required amounts--- then the pudding *is* sour! Something is wrong in the kitchen!

You can't just casually dismiss the negative reactions as people who just have bad tastes! Either your recipe is bad, or the way the pudding was cooked was bad, or the manner in which the food was prepared or presented was at fault! Whatever, you---as the Chief Chef--are responsible! Rather than try to force-feed your people sour pudding, work on the System and its constituent Processes to make things better!

This is what "Godly Quality Management" is all about! "Quality" is that which well-meets your "customer's" desired objective. In that definition, Quality is in the eyes (or mouth) of the customer! Unfortunately, this is part of the resistance that many church leaders hold to the idea of Quality: *that it doesn't matter if the people like or don't like what is done at church*!

Under this mindset everything at church is being done to please God: when in fact, church is a mechanism from God to help *us*! But the attitude "This is exactly how God wants it done---and it doesn't matter if you like it or not" short-circuits effective church management.

Church leaders may demonize children, visitors, and even some members for not meekly "falling in line" and "loving" whatever it is that Tradition delivers. But in our society where people can largely make their own decisions and direct their own actions, young people when matured will leave, visitors will only come once, and tired members will drift out the back door!

While it's true that the purpose of a church isn't to superficially-entertain its people, it *SHOULD* be to *EDIFY* (build up) its people! *If the people don't feel they are being built up then they don't feel they are being built up*, no matter how much you preach they should feel otherwise!

"Godly Quality Management" understands good techniques and methods, used by Jesus, that provide individual true edification! Learning the techniques and methods that Jesus exemplified with his followers will get you acquainted and competent with things such as the following: 1) study, 2) self-evaluation, 3) soliciting honest feedback, 4) customer service, 6) facilitation, 7) continual process improvement, 8) system dynamics, 9) training programs, and 10) small-group people-and-process dynamics.

It's like playing tennis. I fancied myself a tennis player. Yes, having played some way back in high school, I knew that I could still swing a racquet and hit a ball over the net. But when I decided after decades of layoff to join a tennis club I quickly discovered in playing with a group of regular members there that I was an *amateur*! Even worse than that, I was *bad*!

Did I quit? No. It was too important to me---and much too much fun to do it to just quit! Instead, I took some lessons from a professional. I self-evaluated. I worked out for weeks and months just with a machine that fired balls at me. I studied articles and books that I purchased from Amazon.com. I went to YouTube.com and looked at a lot of short instructional videos. I went back and tried some more. I took more lessons. I carefully observed the elite players competing in tournaments on TV.

And gradually my skills grew! Suddenly I was aware not just of what I was doing right but what I was unconsciously doing wrong! The results were visible and undeniable. I was hitting the ball better and more consistently. It was starting to make the ball zoom to where I wanted it to go! I was beginning to get the results I wanted!

All of this took a lot of time, effort, and practice. But it all started with *humility*: admitting that I *wasn't* the expert tennis player I thought I was! I needed help from books, from videos, and from professional instructors. Only then could I truly play the game I wanted, "managing" the ball in the *best* way possible!

**Possible Action Items:**
- *Bring in an outside expert* in church functions to conduct a nonbiased, independent evaluation of all your congregational efforts.
- *Put aside your natural defensive reactions* --- carefully considering areas of church function that are poor while holding back your own self-righteous anger.

- *Come up with a plan* to address your congregational deficiencies. Run this by your outside consultant who can give you unbiased advice on its validity.
- *Study how to institute a well-functioning, ongoing feedback solicitation system* --- not just a dusty box on the wall in a corner of the entrance to the church for "suggestions" that nobody uses or checks.
- *Get helpful feedback from your members on an ongoing basis* --- on whether or not what you are doing is actually meeting their valid spiritual needs: plus helpful suggestions for necessary improvements when it isn't.
- *Don't be defensive in facing requested criticism--- rather withhold judgment while offering immediate "Thanks!"* looking not to automatically defend the "status quo" but to making your congregation the best it can be for truly edifying its members.
- *Study articles, books, and videos on Quality Management* --- looking to make your selves ever-better as managers for the Lord.
- *Set aside regular non-rushed periods of relaxed time* for the sole purpose of discussion by the collected leadership of articles, books, and videos on effective church management.
- *Go to seminars and meetings* focused on how to be even better nonprofit, volunteer-group managers.

. . . . . . . . . . . . . . . . . . . . . . . . . . . . . . . . . . . . . . . . . . . . . . . . . . . . .

33) **Know and support the talents of your people, both individually and collectively** --- JESUS KNEW AND SUPPORTED THE TALENTS OF HIS PEOPLE, BOTH INDIVIDUALLY AND COLLECTIVELY!

Most Church of Christ congregational Leaders have little or no idea of the talents, skills, and interest of their members. Why? The main, sad answer is: "They're not interested in knowing." The second contributing answer is that they don't have a means to collect or access that information.

They are not interested in knowing this because their focus is almost entirely on conducting rituals which only require a preacher, a song-leader, and a handful of men to lead prayers or hand out communion. Thus, since almost all the "church time" is taken up with rituals (Sunday morning formal Bible Study Classes, Sunday morning Worship Service, Sunday evening Duplicate Worship Service, and formal midweek Bible Study Classes) there's little or no need for accessing or using individual talents (other than finding a few people to teach the formal children's classes).

With no apparent need for knowing or accessing the talents of one's congregation, it just isn't on the "radar." Even if the leadership should wish to access particular talents there's no mechanism in place to do so. By casual conversation amongst cliques of friends some of this becomes known to the church leaders, but it's more of an accident than a deliberate process.

Other Christian groups, however, not only value but create enabling frameworks to *use* the talents of their members---and have explicit processes in place to gather and access this incredibly useful and valuable information! Indeed, these other Christian groups have a healthy balance of worship, study, and application---all while simultaneously offering the opportunity for close fellowship in small-group environments.

They do not fear, indeed embrace, the concept of effective Programs which need and utilize the talents of their membership. Thus they create a religious environment in which people can worship the Lord joyfully together, find close Christian friendship, and are of real service to others using and growing their unique talents.

When Church of Christ congregations muzzle their women they cripple themselves. When they ignore the vast wealth of talent within their membership in favor of rituals and grade school-level Bible classes, they chop themselves off at the knees. Is it any wonder that mainline Church of Christ congregations typically don't "run"? They can barely crawl, and that going around in circles...

Yes, this is a harsh criticism! I apologize for the offense but not for the observation. It would not be such a sad situation if it occurred just because of ignorance. But Church of Christ leadership typically doesn't *want* to know better! They are happy doing things the easiest, simplest, safest way.

JESUS DID NOT DO THINGS THE EASIEST, SIMPLEST, AND SAFEST WAY! If he'd done like Church of Christ modern-day leadership often does, he'd have stayed safely sequestered at the local synagogue sitting in silence listening to the Priests, accepting the writings of the Scribes, and conforming to all the stifling requirements and rules of the Pharisees---all while ignoring and suppressing his own God-given incredibly-great Talents!

This is a main reason why many Church of Christ members feel ignored and suppressed. Out of their great love for God these demotivated members put up with the imposed, traditional, and minimally-useful or even painfully-negative rituals...out of a sense of duty.

But just think how much better things might be if the Church Leaders decided to know the full talents of their people and find good ways to help them to work together to use them to the benefit of each other and the congregation! It would be a revolution of productivity to the glory of God and credit to the local congregation.

The saddest thing is that it's not unusual for the lips of preachers and Bible teachers to speak the right words urging us to use our talents in service to others as our Godly duty and joy...which words are then *stifled* by the lack of necessary management efforts to actually facilitate or help accomplish those wonderful objectives!

**Possible Action Items:**
- *Search online for good survey tools* to access the skills, talents, and desires for service in your membership.
- In person, by mail, or online *solicit all the membership to participate* in the selected survey.
- Put the solicited key information into *selected, purchased, excellent church-management software* --- which can then be used by leadership and members for setting up and running small-group Bible Action Groups.
- *Periodically repeat* the survey.
- Have *an excellent visitor-visitation program* where anyone that comes to the church building is quickly visited --- taking a brief initial survey of their interests and talents.
- Regularly hold a leadership meeting---or defined committee---that has the sole purpose of *considering if the talents of the membership are being well-utilized* and if the valid spiritual interests of the people are being met in Bible Action Groups. If the answer is "no" then necessary adjustments are proposed for: 1) dropping minimally-productive activities; 2)

modifying existing activities; or 3) adding new activities.
- *Appoint a Quality Committee* --- that has the ongoing purpose of considering if the talents of the membership are being well-utilized and if the valid spiritual interests of the people are being met in Bible Action Groups.

..................................................

34) **Institute effective training programs** --- JESUS PERSONALLY TRAINED HIS DISCIPLES, TAKING THEM WITH HIM AND DIRECTLY INVOLVING THEM IN HIS EVANGELISTIC CAMPAIGNS!

A well-known admonition in the Bible is to teach people who are then able to teach other people...and so on! This is a potent example of the importance of in-house training programs. Although you might think it's "obvious" how to do some particular task, it's not.

When I am training a person in some task I go through three discrete steps: 1) show it to them by me doing it and them watching, explaining what I do as I go along, telling them to not worry about the details just get the "overview" in their mind; 2) them do it as I am there constantly explaining and directing; and 3) them do it as I am close at hand, available to help if there's any question or problem.

I vividly remember working in a reference microbial-pathogen-identification military laboratory when I was in the U.S. Air Force. A group of people training to identify in their own smaller labs the "bad bugs" came in. One of our higher sergeants "trained" them in a particular procedure. To my eyes he was visibly arrogant and intimidated by one of the lower-ranking personnel (like me, not in the military because he wanted to be there, but was forced by our "Uncle Sam" to do so) who held a doctorate, Ph.D. degree!

Anyway, the "trainer" ran through a quick, glib explanation of the procedure then said: "Now you do it!" The complicated procedure was such that even I, who had worked in that lab for a year or so, wouldn't know how to do it! But the trainees did as ordered, giving it their best---until a test tube filled with bacteria slipped out of the hands of the Ph.D. fellow, falling to the floor! The sergeant with clear contempt and glee said "Don't move!" and sterilized the floor around their feet before cleaning up the broken glass, gloating in his "superiority"!

Was this effective training? No! But in this military situation where one is the superior and the others are the inferiors, you cannot raise an objection! In the Church of Christ where a common tradition is "submission" to those "in authority," objecting to unworkable or incomplete direction is likewise not done!

The most glaring example of this sad situation is the admonition from the pulpit to "Go out and just tell people what Jesus has done for you!"---a command that has either zero or a negative effect on people! This is what is called "arrogant preaching of superiority" that none of our friends or relatives "out in the world" would sit still for! Yet the preacher persists, smug in his attitude of superior knowledge legislating to "bad" people who he deems as too selfish to just "talk to people about Jesus as if He were your new grandchild!"

Congregations of the Church of Christ just sit in bored silence as the preacher predictably harangues them. They'd like to tell the preacher and other congregational leadership to go down the street and "benchmark" the different Christian group that's there which somehow knows how to put together an active, effective, community-outreach program. But they don't.

They understand that raising that logical objection and practical suggestion for improvement would be futile, labeling them in the eyes of the leadership as (at best) "troublemakers" to be leery of, or (at worst) "heretics"---to be marginalized and/or pushed out of the congregation!

Instead of spouting empty slogans, *TRAIN* people in effective methods! Of course this would mean: 1) having a defined, effective program into which to train people; 2) having trainers who know how to *effectively* teach a subject; and 3) have trainers who actually know how to effectively do that task!

But since it is common in mainline Church of Christ congregations for none of this to be present, training is largely absent. However, this situation could easily be reversed if: 1) the leadership gets more serious about the work of the church in general; and 2) they get more serious at finding methods that truly work at achieving desired specific objectives.

Every "program" that works does so not by accident or sloppy attempts but by "professional" attention to details! Conducting a ritual is easy. Gearing up a program to effectively address a specific need is difficult. *Keeping* that effective program running into the future is even more difficult. But the key to having an expanding rather than contracting congregation is to train people in effective procedures who are then competent to effectively train others.

**Possible Action Steps:**
- *Identify desired objectives* for the congregation which are presently not being met or are being met poorly. Prioritize these objectives.
- *Bring in an outside, expert consultant* to help put together an ongoing program which effectively meets the desired top-priority objective (such as establishing a successful small-group, in-home, weekly sermon-discussion program).
- Have the outside consultant *train the initial participants* in their particular roles, duties, and procedures.
- Then have the outside consultant who is expert in the area being addressed help *put together an "in-house" ongoing training program* to keep the training going into the future: such as periodic formal short (one or two day) courses, or online videos, or "apprenticeships."

- Each person in a formal "job" is asked to *find an interested person to be his or her "assistant"* who is then trained via O.J.T ("on-the-job training").
- Ministers at every opportunity, or other church leaders doing "church" tasks *take along someone as a helper* who is then trained by O.J.T. to eventually take over that task him-or-herself (who then takes along someone else, training them in turn...and so on!).
- In every situation *consider if this is an opportunity to help other people express their talents*: teaching and enthusing them by active involvement!
- Preachers especially can *train others through meaningful involvement*: such as asking Bible classes to have their kids help to put together requested specific visuals for projection in the sermon, or writing short poems that express particular points, or penning short essays of examples to be read in sermons and classes, etc.
- Song leaders or music directors could ask for *original words or actual new songs* on particular topics coming up in the congregational study program.

. . . . . . . . . . . . . . . . . . . . . . . . . . . . . . . . . . . . . . . . . . . . . . . . . . . . . . . . .

35) **In ways that do not needlessly offend people, provide opportunity for personal growth, meaningful service, and productive fun** --- JESUS PROVIDED FOR HIS FOLLOWERS OPPORTUNITY FOR PERSONAL GROWTH, MEANINGFUL SERVICE, AND PRODUCTIVE FUN!

Disrupting the expected, traditional ritual services needlessly can be very disturbing to the congregation. Any changes, no matter how slight, need to be carefully explained in advance, promoted, and supported.

However, don't be afraid to add new things! Just because something is new or different does not make it automatically bad! JESUS ROUTINELY "BROKE THE MOLD" OF THE TRADITIONAL JEWISH PRACTICES OF HIS TIME!

Your people in your congregation have an inward need not just for ritualistic worship services but also for meaningful close fellowship and productive, enjoyable service! If you offer the opportunity for people to address together a specific identified need, all sorts of good ideas and approaches will emerge!

Unfortunately, Church of Christ leadership has the misplaced idea that they need to be the ones handing-down the answers to specific problems or opportunities. No, you don't! You need to be the managers who "facilitate" people bringing you good options from which you, as the appointed decision-makers, make the final decision!

Also "fun" is not a "four-letter" bad word! Yes, "you're not in the business of entertainment," as goes the commonly-stated excuse for boring preaching, boring classes, and boring services. But you ARE in the business of meaningful enlightenment---which *needs* to be truly *interesting* to be effective!

In other words, services, sermons, and classes need to *not* be painful chores! Getting like-interested, talented people together for moderated discussion (versus a disrespectful lecture by me where I arrogantly assume that I know people's individual spiritual needs) can be very enjoyable!

Appoint small-group committees to research and come up with good options on specific tasks! Facilitate them so that they function smoothly. Again, this can be very enjoyable to the people involved---if it's smooth and productive! Of course, you as the appointed church leadership make the final decision on everything, so everything remains in good control.

What you are doing with well-commissioned "work groups" is "making a space" for Godly Creativity! This is not a threat to your control or doctrines. This is not a threat to your beloved rituals. Nothing is done or changed without your approval.

Yes, I know that it is scary and somewhat dangerous to encourage people to think on their own. But it can be tremendously effective because when you as the appointed leadership make the final decision you already have what's called "buy-in" where the people who gave you those options: where they have already invested their own interest into the subject!

How many times have you deliberated on your own handed down a mandate, seen people dutifully nod in agreement, and nothing happens? How many times have you made some decision, had it announced from the pulpit, and seen zero participation? Delegate a little authority to a committee or work group to come up with good options and you may see much more enthusiasm and participation!

But it *does* take a *change of perspective*, from "Defend the Truth!" to "*Help* your people to *DO* the Truth!" Provide encouragement, a clear mandate, and strong ongoing support! Then you can step back and keep a close watch on the great things that are happening! If things start going "off track" you can step in and help keep the "train" in motion!

Truly being good Managers of excellent programs that people want to be part has great benefits: 1) it grows their talents, 2) it is enjoyable, and 3) it produces results that the participants are proud to be part of!

**Possible Action Items:**
- *Consider how you can help your people grow, use their talents, and have fun* outside sitting listening to lectures---without regard as to any particular option's feasibility or practicality.
- *Consider good criteria for ranking the possibilities* one against the other (such as cost, number of people involved, importance of the problem/opportunity being addressed, how well it will help people grow their talents, how enjoyable it will be to the participants, etc.)
- *Select the top one or two priorities* based on your good criteria---and commission a committee or Action Group to make specific plans on how to accomplish them.
- *Pilot-test, improve and then roll-out* to the general congregation the new program or activity.
- *Get feedback on its effectiveness* both from participants and customers, using that information to continue, discontinue, or improve the program.
- *Put out a survey to members* on what they'd like to see as improvements or additions to the church activities. Do not reject out-of-hand any of the suggestions; rather, consider the underlying valid spiritual needs prompting that particular suggestion.
- *Go to other congregations of the Church of Christ that are running programs you might like to have at*

*your congregation,* to talk to their leadership and participants on how they made them work.
- *Go visit other Christian groups that are running programs you might like to have at your congregation,* to see what might be applicable to your group and how to make them work.
- *Seriously consider whether your existing efforts and any new ones will help your membership grow their talents, serve actual customers, and are enjoyable to the participants* --- improving or replacing any activities that fail to meet these minimal requirements.

..............................................................

36) **"Up your game" as successes produce fruit** --- JESUS DEALT WITH HIS DISCIPLES AND FOLLOWERS DIFFERENTLY AS HE ACHIEVED GREATER SUCCESS, MOVING FROM TACTICAL TO STRATEGIC OBJECTIVES!

Many a Church of Christ congregation that was "on a roll"---helping its members to grow their talents, to serve actual grateful customers, and to provide deep enjoyment to all participants---has *CRASHED AND BURNED!*

If you've been in the Church of Christ long enough, it's likely you observed or were part of a growing congregation that suddenly shrank from a couple hundred down to a couple dozen people! And no, it wasn't because Satan saw you succeeding and stepped in to gum things up! It was likely because your appointed leadership could not make the transition from a small to a large congregation.

Just as in a business setting, the leadership has to "up their game" when transitioning from a "Mom and Pop" operation to a bigger organization! Leadership must back off from tactical control (being directly in charge of and participating in all the functions) to more strategic management! Indeed, "management" must become true "leadership"----setting the direction and priorities rather than directly overseeing the day-to-day operations.

This is very difficult for Church of Christ leaders who typically have little or no training in running nonprofit, volunteer organizations. It's not so hard to manage a small congregation where everyone knows everyone and tasks are done by mostly the same small group of people. In a larger organization (above 100 adult members) it suddenly becomes difficult to know or keep track of everyone, be on top of each activity, and even have the time to keep up with what's going on!

For those church leaders who think it'll be just "more of the same" they likely will quickly be swamped and overwhelmed. Falling back on old habits of trying to figure it all out themselves, the leadership of the congregation is confused and desperate as the congregation quickly becomes partitioned and fragmented---setting the stage for "splits" where dissatisfied people go elsewhere.

It's not just "playing the game better" that's necessary when true growth occurs---it's having the courage and wisdom to change to a new, more-complicated sport! It's like going from golf to basketball! There are new rules! There is new complexity! The goals have changed! And the coaches need to learn new things, acquire new skills, and set their sights higher!

So in the rare occasion where your good-management efforts bear fruit, don't just sit back on your laurels! Get outside consultation, collectively read and discuss more key books, and improve your church communication and oversight functions! Don't let your success be your undoing!

**Possible Action Items:**
- *Adopt the attitude of "continual learning"* in your management efforts.
- *Know that you will never reach a plateau* where you can sit back, relax, and let good programs just proceed on "autopilot."
- *Keep up a self-training regular schedule* where you together with the other church leaders set aside a regular time for only study and growth (no regular business allowed!): bringing in guest speakers, together reading and discussing new management books, going to visit other places.
- *Resist the urge to hand down ill-considered, "knee-jerk" reactions* --- moving beyond "I like it/I don't like it" or "It's right/It's wrong" to a careful evaluation

based on clear desired criteria backed up with real data (numbers).
- *Bring in outside consultants* when you hit new plateaus or fresh challenges rather than just automatically thinking: "We can figure this out on our own!"
- *Keep the overall Objective clearly in mind* --- a clearly-articulated Vision of what you want to achieve: trumping feelings of comfort, territoriality, or defensiveness.

------------------------------------------------

### Chapter Six:

## CHURCH LEADERSHIP

37) **Stop thinking that you are perfect** --- JESUS EXCORIATED THE RELIGIOUS LEADERSHIP OF HIS TIME FOR THINKING THAT THEY WERE PERFECT IN EVERY WAY!

"Leadership" is part of Management. But Leadership is *not* Management. Management has to do with directing the everyday operations. Leadership has to do with *where* you are trying to go!

By definition, as a religious group you're not where you want to go! Many Church of Christ congregations make the mistake of thinking that they've already arrived at a state of perfect that only needs to be maintained. Yet the membership is incessantly accused by Preachers of not going out and evangelizing the world! Make up your mind! Are you perfect or are you far from perfect?

The answer, of course, is in the middle. No matter how well you do things, it's always possible to do things better. JESUS MOVED RELENTLESSLY FORWARD. Jesus' *AIM* was, indeed, to help mankind move closer to God!

When one's vision is shifted from methods to goals, it is obvious that Church of Christ congregations are far from perfect. Yet Church of Christ leadership seems obsessed with maintaining present methods (mainly traditional rituals *not* mandated in the New Testament) while ignoring the overriding goals of Jesus! This shortsightedness is part of the problem that cripples many Church of Christ congregations, setting them up for stagnation and shrinkage.

Thinking they are the perfect reflection of "The New Testament Church" leaves no room for improvement! Mainline

Church of Christ leaders need to acknowledge that the actual "New Testament" congregations of Christians described in the New Testament scriptures failed in many ways!

But helpful criticism unfortunately runs up not just against the doctrine of perfection, but personal egos. When the congregation is in obvious decline, pointing out faults becomes a personal affront to the appointed leadership! It's quite true that *for feedback to be helpful it must be sincerely requested by leadership*!

No Church of Christ I've ever been part of has an effective means to solicit requested feedback. Therefore you can't say anything!

This doctrine of perfection, this natural defensive attitude, this lack of any official way to provide safe feedback---all conspire to prevent congregations from making any forward progress! Before any reversal of the steady decline can be achieved, *LEADERSHIP MUST BECOME HUMBLE*!

JESUS THE SON OF GOD, IN MANY WAYS AND EXAMPLES, TOOK UPON HIMSELF A TRUE ATTITUDE OF HUMILITY!

This necessary humility cannot be just an affected "ah shucks I'm just one of the guys" attitude. It has to be a policy carried out by real mechanisms. It must acknowledge that we're not where we want to be! It must admit that the Church of Christ traditional methods are not connecting with the people of this generation! It must agonize over losing one's own children when they mature and quit or go elsewhere! And it must obsess over generating true joy and interest in its own membership to come to the church and participate!

From that perspective of humility, Godly Wise Leaders can then struggle with finding and implementing workable solutions to these over-riding Problems, thus truly leading the membership to move ever-closer to God!

Church management of the status quo is easy in comparison to being Godly Wise Leaders. Keeping things the same as always is safe, simple, and easy. Striving to figure out good ways to move ever-closer to God is complicated, difficult, and even dangerous.

**Possible Action Items:**
- Ask the question: *"What are we trying to achieve?"*
- Ask the question: *"Based on real numbers, are we succeeding?"*
- Ask the question: *"If we're not where we want to be, how can we improve our methods* to better meet our goals?"
- Ask the question: *"Is it possible for us to be more like Jesus?"*
- Ask the question: *"In what specific ways* might be try to be more like Jesus?"
- Ask the question: *"Are we teaching Jesus in word and deed to our young people,* as our top teaching priority?"
- Ask the question: "When visitors come to church *are they seeing Jesus in word and in action?"*
- Ask the question: "As the appointed leaders, *are we helping our members to be more like Jesus* in thought, word, and action?"
- Ask the question: *"Is Jesus the center* of our doctrines, sermons, and classes?"
- Ask the question: *"Do we know and teach the Radical Principles* of Jesus?
- Ask the question: *"Does the community around us see Jesus* in word and action, or just another church building?"
- Ask the question: *"How might we better show to our community Jesus* in word and action?"

- Ask the question: *"Which of Jesus' methods can we adopt or better-emulate in our community, today?"*
..............................................

38) **Stop thinking that you can't learn anything from others** --- JESUS HONORED JOHN THE BAPTIST; JESUS ADAPTED HIS STRATEGY TO THE LOCAL SITUATION; AND JESUS CHALLENGED HIS FOLLOWERS TO THINK OUTSIDE THEIR PRESENT "RELIGIOUS BOX"!

By definition, Leadership goes beyond management in taking their people to places they've not gone before.

From the paradigm of "feed and protect the flock," *real* shepherds of flocks of sheep *can't* stay in the same meadow indefinitely! The local food sources are consumed. To stay further is to starve the sheep. The wise shepherd must be constantly figuring out how to move his flock to a new site where the grass is plentiful and fresh.

So also must Wise Godly Leaders seek to keep their congregation healthy by not allowing the message---or methods of delivery of the message---to stagnate. Stagnation leads to lethargy which leads to spoiling which leads to disease which leads to death.

While the message of Jesus certainly doesn't change, the delivery thereof must be allowed to adjust to the changing needs of your community and society.

In my experience, Church of Christ preachers and leaders even confuse the message itself, often substituting traditional doctrine as the focus instead of Jesus.

Fortunately however, Jesus' teachings and examples aren't "yes-or-no", "right-or-wrong" absolute rules ("doctrines"). Instead, they are dynamic Principles which cover all present and future situations!

Yes, there's a verse in the Bible that says to follow the "Apostle's Doctrines"---but were those not the Principles of Jesus?

Should not the "Apostle's Doctrines" remain the same today, as the Teachings of Jesus?

Beyond that, Jesus' teachings and examples of how to implement them are RADICAL! For instance, it's not just "try to be nice to people who are nice to you" but "show true love by your actions even to enemies trying to kill you!" Being a bit nicer to people in general is something quite reasonable and ordinary. Loving by real actions people trying to kill you is extreme and even bizarre!

But instead of wrestling with these incredibly difficult concepts from Jesus, many Church of Christ congregations are so sunk into their traditional beliefs and practices that they can't even recognize the need to struggle!

But if they'd just look around their own community, they'd see examples of other religious groups proving by their ongoing actions that it is possible to do better for Jesus and God than the isolated, in-grown Church of Christ congregations are doing!

*Godly Wise Leadership sees beyond the individual trees to the forest*! Godly Wise Leadership isn't afraid to adopt a Vision that's greater than just maintaining the stifling status quo! Godly Wise Leadership doesn't throw up their hands in defeat but finds good, acceptable ways attempting to move forward to do ever-better for Jesus and God! Godly Wise Leadership adopts a humble attitude willing and even *eager* to learn how to do better than they've previously done!

You are not perfect. Your methods are not perfect. Your doctrines are not perfect. Your congregation is not perfect. There *is* room to do better!

I believe that God will judge us not only on if we've fought hard to maintain that which works, but if we've had the courage to strive to be and do ever-better!

**Possible Action Items:**
- *Admit where you're not succeeding* as well as you would like.
- *Prioritize* the most urgent items needing fixing/improving.
- *Appoint committees* to study the top two or three problems and submit back to you several options for each problem (with strengths and weaknesses to each possible solution) for fixing them.
- *Educate yourselves* better --- as to how to successfully lead people in implementing new solutions to high-priority problems (by studying key books, articles, and videos).
- *Bring in advisors* --- who are acknowledged experts in understanding and implementing solutions to your identified key problems.
- *Go to other congregations* of the Church of Christ where they have solved those particular problems to find out what they did and if it might work for you.
- *Visit neighboring Christian groups* --- where they have solved similar problems; to find out if some of their techniques and methods might work for you.
- *Carefully implement desired programs* that will overcome problems in moving your people closer to God --- looking to pilot-test, evaluate, improve, and test again before rolling them out to the congregation with strong explanation, promotion, and support.

. . . . . . . . . . . . . . . . . . . . . . . . . . . . . . . . . . . . . . . . . . . . .

39) **Make it easy for people to provide helpful feedback** --- JESUS PUBLICLY ENGAGED WITH BOTH CRITICS AND ENEMIES!

Wise Godly Leadership wants to know the *EFFECTIVENESS* of what they are doing! They don't just hand down decisions from on high with the attitude: "If you like it, great---but if you don't like it, too bad!"

People that feel their good ideas, talents, and skills are not needed will logically but silently respond: *"Fine! You didn't need my input or response, so go your own way! Since you obviously don't need my good ideas, talents, or skills then do it yourself! Maybe you're the 'authority' to which I must 'submit', but my participation will be the bare minimum, if that! I can clearly see that you are happily "driving the car off the cliff," but if you don't want my feedback then have fun falling down and killing yourself!"*

Wow! That's harsh, isn't it? But that is exactly what the church leadership gets when it actively or passively ignores the feedback of its membership.

"But we're the Leaders!" they might angrily assert. "We're supposed to lead and they are supposed to follow! How dare they get mad at us for doing our job?"

Wise Godly Leadership (indeed all wise leadership) ignores their own people at their own peril. First of all, there's no "buy-in" to enthusiastically participate, when some decision is "handed down from above" with no or little input from those expected to implement the decision. Second, "the best laid plans of mice and men often go astray." To keep even an excellent plan on track you must have constant feedback on how well that plan is doing, making careful adjustments as you proceed!

Ignoring the true spiritual needs of your people gets exactly what many Church of Christ congregations are facing today, namely: 1) loss of one's youth, 2) loss of existing members, and 3) failure to engage visitors.

Now, not only must Wise Godly Leaders be open to feedback: "Anyone can talk to me with any concerns!"---they must actually *SOLICIT* and *MAKE IT EASY* for people to give feedback! *"I want your feedback and here's the good mechanism to provide it!"* Unless you *ask* for helpful criticism, people will just keep their mouths shut---shrugging their shoulders sadly as you drive off that proverbial cliff!
And unless you make it easy for people to give helpful criticism, people will not go to the bother or trouble!

I'm reminded of the story of a top American car company that was having trouble selling its cars. People down on the shop floor were complaining bitterly about ancient broken machinery, poor inspection of products, shoddy parts supplied from subcontractors, and poor working conditions. At the very same time that this was common knowledge amongst the workers, the leadership at the top floor of their corporate headquarters was widely bragging to the news media: "We sell the best damn cars in America!"

Modern-day car companies know full well if they ignore the feedback from their customers *and* employees they will perish! The car companies instituted (made part of the regular way that business is done) a number of good processes to actively get feedback (whether positive or negative) from both their external and internal customers. Yes, even their employees were now regarded as "customers" (those inside the organization) to whom the leadership is responsible! That's Wise Leadership.

Now, Church of Christ congregations are handicapped by a misunderstanding of the verse that says we aren't to preach to "itching ears." Sure, the Gospel isn't something to adjust to the whims and feelings of the particular congregation's membership. But that's not what we're discussing here! That scripture is a "red herring" that misleads leadership! That verse in the Bible is not a license to bore people, to ignore their valid spiritual needs, nor sidetrack the talents of one's people!

I'm reminded of the account of a young minister who agreed to be hired into a dying congregation to try and help them out. Their "midweek Bible study" was a church leader who'd been there for many years, who had everyone (meaning a handful of dutifully-suffering members) get down on their knees, close their eyes, and bow as he lead them in an hour-long "prayer"!

Being a cooperative, respectful person, the newly-hired minister got down on his knees, closed his eyes, folded his hands together and endured the pain of that position while inevitably drifting off to sleep---just like the handful of other incredibly-dedicated members present. Needless to say, that young minister did not stay there long, but found a way to go elsewhere at his first opportunity!

Maybe the sermon monologue disguised as a prayer was saying some good things, but the *METHOD* was incredibly painful and ineffective! JESUS WAS NOT AN INEFFECTIVE SPEAKER IGNORING THE VALID SPIRITUAL NEEDS OF HIS AUDIENCE!

If that church leader had ever allowed safe feedback, he'd have discovered that the methodology he used at those services was atrociously bad! But apparently he didn't care. Likely his true, deepest motivation was to be the center of attention rather than do what would truly help his people move closer to God.

**Possible Action Items:**
- *Study how to structure and implement a workable feedback program* --- buying key up-to-date books on the subject, looking at expert videos, or bringing in someone who elsewhere already runs an effective feedback program.
- *Put response cards in the pews* --- with two key questions on the back: 1) "What did we do today that met your spiritual needs?" and 2) "How might we do better at meeting your valid spiritual needs?" To make this overt criticism palatable to leadership, you might also include a third question: "What prayer requests do you have for our prayer group to take before God." Thus it can be called a "Prayer Request Card" that also gathers helpful feedback. Collect them in the contribution trays along with the donated money, evaluate them carefully, and implement improvements where feasible---while passing on to the prayer group any prayer requests.
- *Send out a regularly-timed, well-written survey* --- perhaps once per year to the entire congregation so everyone knows that you are seriously looking for their suggestions and help for keeping good things while improving where needed!
- *Off-the-record, quietly sit down and talk in private with key people* not part of the appointed leadership: asking them confidentially what's going well, what's going wrong, and what improvement might be helpful.
- *Have a "suggestion box" where people can leave anonymous feedback at any time* --- or, if they wish, can include their contact information for actual responses. If contact information is left, then within a short time send a "thank you" card appreciating their concern and stating that their suggestion(s) are being seriously considered.
- *If you receive a good idea, publicly acknowledge it with thanks* --- call them up and talk with them in

person on their ideas for implementation if there is contact information available. It it's a bad idea, simply send another card saying something like: "we're not able to do this at this time but will keep it in mind for the future. We appreciate your interest and look forward to getting more ideas from you!"
- *Have Quality Response Short Surveys for actual customers*, just like the best online business sites have, to make sure your good objectives are actually being met.

. . . . . . . . . . . . . . . . . . . . . . . . . . . . . . . . . . . . . . . . . . . . . . . . . . . .

40) **Recognize that church-leadership is not primarily providing stability ("more of the same") but rather is a demanding position which requires Continual Learning** --- JESUS DID NOT ORDER THE THOUSANDS ATTENDING HIS EVENTS TO MEEKLY RETURN TO THEIR SYNAGOGUES TO BE LECTURED YET AGAIN, FOR THE 10,000$^{th}$ TIME, ON THE LIFE OF ABRAHAM!

It is very easy and attractive to think that we are perfect in every way. Why? Because then there is zero need to have to study, struggle, and improve!

Religion, where many people are "in" it for spiritual reassurance, loves to "attain" unto perfection. It is the rare group that does not assert they are the "true" church! This perfection is then "certified" by being exactly (preaching and doing) what *God* demands from us---whether or not the Founder or Holy Scriptures would agree!

The next step on the road to perfection is to demonize anything different. We, therefore, are not only doing what we feel is best, but what is *right*! Other people doing something different are not merely doing things in a less-than-best way, but are *wrong*!

Furthermore, by them not accepting what we "know" to be mandated from God---they are proving themselves evil heretics consciously "thumbing their noses" at God! Therefore it is fine not just to separate from them and feel superior to them but to do anything at all to punish them! After all, are they not "evil demons" who have denied God by not doing all the details that God supposedly requires of them?!

This, then, is the source of intra-and-inter-religious bitter conflict and war: where people actually take up weapons to slaughter and kill each other! And it all starts with the attitude that we are God's chosen people doing everything perfectly as He wants it!

JESUS MOVED PEOPLE BEYOND THE CONCEPT OF PERFECTION TO *STRUGGLE*!

Where the Jewish Priests, Scribes, and Pharisees of Jesus' time insisted on exactly how God wanted people to follow Him in all circumstances in every detail, JESUS TAUGHT SPIRITUAL FREEDOM---ROOTED NOT IN ANYONE DOING ANYTHING THEY WANTED, BUT IN THE PERSONAL CHALLENGE OF LIVING UP TO RADICAL PRINCIPLES!

Now I've mentioned this concept previously in this book. I bring it up again to make the critical point that the concept of personal responsibility in struggling with radical Jesus-principles must start with the appointed Leadership!

This is not a "management" issue of getting and keeping some program chugging along! This is truly a JESUS-LEADERSHIP ISSUE---where the Leadership must "set the tone" to which the whole congregation dances! If your attitude is "we are perfect in every way!"---then anything otherwise will be scoffed-at, belittled, denied, and rejected.

Personal, congregational, and leadership JESUS-STIMULATED STRUGGLE is when we *truly* follow Jesus! Thinking you've got everything down perfectly is following the Jewish leaders of Jesus' time who *killed* Jesus!

Yes, I agree this is a difficult concept! But let's go back, again, to just *what* are we following? Are we Christians who above all else are following Jesus---or are we simply "apologists" who are mindlessly defending our handed-down beliefs and practices?

I stress again that Godly Wise Leadership, of course, does not throw out one's traditional beliefs or practices for no reason. This would be very traumatic to one's congregation, the main fault of so-called "liberals" who try to improve things but instead fail miserably.

But where there is good reason to improve something for Jesus and God (in order to connect to your community, inspire your young people, intrigue visitors, and keep your members), Wise Godly Leadership carefully explains, advertises in advance, promotes, and carefully implements any changes to the "status quo."

But *WHERE PEOPLE UNDERSTAND THE VISION OF JESUS AND HOW THE IMPROVEMENTS WILL FURTHER ACHIEVING THAT VISION* the congregation will happily follow where its Leadership leads it---particularly if doing so engenders true joyful growth through meaningful service and close fellowship!

Leadership is about Vision. Is Jesus the center of your vision for your congregation? And, is this "Jesus" who is at the center of your Vision THE REAL JESUS WHO NOT ONLY TAKES THE CRUSHING BURDENS OF LIFE OFF OUR OWN SHOULDERS, LOVES US, AND SAVES US---BUT WHO REQUIRES STRUGGLE IMPLEMENTING HIS RADICAL PRINCIPLES: CALLING US TO PRODUCTIVE SACRIFICE, DEMANDING THAT WE LIFT UP OUR OWN CROSS AND ACTIVELY FOLLOW IN HIS BLOODY FOOTSTEPS?

Yes, that Vision is complicated, hard, and dangerous. *It is much easier instead of following in the LEADERSHIP EXAMPLE OF JESUS to be mere managers of tradition.* Let us be brave enough and wise enough to carefully take the nobler path.

**Possible Action Items:**
- Have a *leadership retreat* focused not on management business but on Vision.
- In a paragraph or less, describe *where you want your congregation to go* (your Vision) in your community.
- *Determine the "center" of your Vision* around which all else revolves or upon which it all depends (your "AIM"---the center of your target, the Vision).
- Clearly articulate your *AIM in five words or less* for your congregation.
- Under the AIM put *up to five main Goals.*
- *Under each Goal put up to five main Objectives.*
- Ask the question: "*How might we better-achieve* these objectives, goals, AIM, and Vision?
- Where you are clearly falling well-short, for the top one-to-three priorities, *appoint committees* to bring back practical suggestions for improvement, for further evaluation by the appointed leadership.
- For approved plans carefully prepare the congregation, telling them you'll do a "test" first before anything is permanent. Do the Pilot testing plus evaluation plus improvement: then *roll out to the congregation* the improvement. The "roll-out" is done with all necessary explanations, advertisements, promotions, preparation, training, and ongoing strong support.
- At least once every few years *repeat* the above!

..............................................................

41) **Voluntarily expand the leadership base** --- JESUS EXPANDED RELIGIOUS LEADERSHIP FAR BEYOND THE ACCEPTED CATEGORIES OF HIS TIME!
A key problem in Church of Christ congregations is that the leadership feels they must come up with all the decisions. This is caused by the doctrine that each congregation must be separate and autonomous (a proscription which is not found in the New Testament). Since no Church of Christ hierarchy exists, there's simply nowhere else to go for input!

Also, they have an extreme reluctance to acknowledge or accept any leadership authority beyond that explicitly spelled out in the New Testament, namely Elders and Deacons (local Ministers are also *not* explicitly approved in the New Testament, but are tacitly accepted as part of the leadership by traditional momentum).

But Wise Godly Leadership recognizes its shortcomings and isolation---and is able to reach outside the congregation for support, while simultaneously nurturing leadership inside.

Unfortunately, to admit they need help is to admit personal weakness! These men see themselves as the Leaders that other people lean upon! Plus, they are all *men* like me---who just naturally have a male problem in "asking for directions," even under the best of circumstances!

So they "soldier on" doing the best they can under the circumstance, never having built up an internal or external leadership support network for when times inevitably go bad! Even under the *best* of all circumstances, an extended leadership support-network is still necessary---such as if the congregation were in a growth phase: where a mere handful of men cannot "cover all the bases" anymore!

Wise Godly Leadership must learn how to delegate authority, turning over some leadership and management duties to others inside the congregation, while welcoming and seeking external advice for dealing with both unexpected problems and unanticipated opportunities.

**Possible Action Items:**
- Set up a *quarterly Church Leadership forum*: where in a wide range of area covering large and small mainline Church of Christ congregations you can rotate a relaxed, couple-hour or half-way meeting on leadership and management issues;
- Regularly delegate authority to well-commissioned, *tightly-mandated research committees* on specific problems or opportunities, for coming up with good options for the appointed leadership to consider.
- *Appoint a "Quality Council"* that meets regularly to determine if the talents of the membership are being best-utilized by church programs; offering suggestions on needed improvements or possible new workgroups for leadership evaluation and approval.
- Ask the ladies to meet monthly at the same time as the "men's business meeting" for a *Women's Work Meeting*, to plan and coordinate the expression together of their many talents; where any programs or efforts coming out of their regular, sanctioned meeting are presented to the appointed leadership for final approval.
- Take advantage of the nonprofit organization legal requirements to have a *board of directors* (which is usually solely composed by the appointed church leadership of Elders and Deacons) to add key people into that forum to give you additional leadership input; where the Elders and Deacons use the expanded board as an additional leadership resource.
- Reach out to local experts in nonprofit, volunteer organization leadership within your community--- establishing *a local advisory board* that meets periodically and is available as needed (possibly giving them a paid stipend for their time and concern).

- Go to existing *local religious leadership forums* across religious groups: not to give approval to their differing activities/beliefs, but to gain insights into the things they do which work better than what you are doing.
- Reach out to interest people across the world willing to be part of a *virtual advisory board* for your congregation; who would meet periodically online and also be just an email away for advice as needed.
- *READ BOOKS* on leadership, sharing the contents with each other, discussing the implications thereof for your congregation.

..................................................

42) **Voluntarily institute and accept "term limits"** --- JESUS' PURPOSE WAS NOT TO BECAME THE PERMANENT RULER OF A SMALL GROUP OF FOLLOWERS, BUT TO FULFILL HIS MANDATE AND THEN STEP ASIDE.

The New Testament neither mandates a life-time term as a church leader nor a set, short period of time. To impose a term limit, might be questioned. But if the appointed leadership were to voluntarily accept a term limit, then why would that be wrong? So why then should you as the appointed leadership consider *voluntarily* instituting a term limit?

It's been my experience that there are two big problems with life-time appointments for church leaders in the Church of Christ: 1) those men who turn out to be poor or bad in the position can drive down the enthusiasm of the congregation who feel a responsibility to either "submit" to "authority" or quit; and 2) inevitable problems and headaches of church management and leadership often cause people to either keep going when they're past their talent limits or to "flame out" causing even more problems.

If Elders and Deacons took upon themselves a staggered term limit (say from 1-3 years to start with for each person, such that each year one or more would come up for a validation election while leaving 2/3 of them in place for continuity) then they'd know they weren't stuck in the job forever and would have a time when they could gracefully retire, having done their duty!

Furthermore, the congregation would have a means to peacefully disapprove people not living up to their job, knowing they'd not "be stuck with forever" people dragging down the congregation.

Also, there are otherwise qualified people who might consider a several-year term as an appointed congregational leader, who would balk at the idea of taking on a lifetime commitment.

**Possible Action Items:**
- *Discuss the possible benefits* of voluntarily instituting a staggered term-limit for your church leaders;
- If you'd like to proceed with this idea, *present to your congregation* the benefits. After they've had time to ask questions and think about it, *take a vote* on it.
- If the congregation agrees to it, *implement the term limits* such that only about a third of the leadership comes up for a renewal, or potential new person to be voted in, each year (so there is a constant overlap of institutional memory and control).

. . . . . . . . . . . . . . . . . . . . . . . . . . . . . . . . . . . . . . . . . . . . . . . . . .

43) **Lead by example but don't think you have to do everything** --- JESUS DELEGATED MANY IMPORTANT JOBS TO HIS DISCIPLES.

Too often the leaders of Church of Christ congregations think that they must always lead by example, taking on the work not only of front-line managers but supervisors and lead workers!

This isn't a bad idea when the congregation is small, composed of only a few dozen people. However, if your congregation were to make some of the improvements I've suggested in previous points and actually start gaining traction---retaining your young people, energizing your members, and converting people of your community---growth will quickly swamp the direct involvement in everything by the leadership!

Furthermore, the main duty of leaders is not to do the "grunt" work, or supervise, or even manage---but to lead! By delegating authority not only are Wise Godly Leaders able to keep on top of what's going on, but they can free up their time to devote their attention to the most important things!

What sort of things? Is the *AIM* of the congregation still valid as the congregation grows larger? Is the congregation still on track to meet the *AIM*, or has it drifted off course? Are the Goals of the congregation still appropriate to the *AIM* and resources of the congregation (you might be able to add some new ones!)? Should some of the Goals be modified or even dropped? For the Goals that do remain valid, are the specific, short-term Objectives being met? Should some Objectives be dropped, modified, or added? Is the larger congregation still operating smoothly or are factions developing? Do you need to step in and remind everyone or particular groups of the *AIM* and Goals? As different interest-groups emerge in the larger congregation do they work in support or opposition to each other? Is a viable, helpful, delegated management structure in place beneath the Appointed Leadership?  Does that delegated management structure communicate well with the people and with the Leadership?  Do you perhaps need to bring in an outside Quality consultant to make sure that you as the Leaders are effectively staying on top of the whole System?  Are you still able to see the entire "forest" or are you getting smothered by the many new "trees"?

Yes, this is a *good* "problem" to have---leading the congregation not just in trying to slow a decline, but in actual growth!  But many Church of Christ congregations on the "up-swing" have been brutally cut-short and *crushed* by inadequate or poor leadership.  Key to maintaining healthy growth is to recognize when it's getting beyond you as a Leader---and finding the needed information or support to quickly get back on top!

Running a nonprofit, volunteer organization is a difficult task---even more difficult than running a for-profit business---in which there is no fault (indeed merit) in quickly reaching out for effective help!

Many times you need only reach deeper into your own organization---by encouragement and strong support---to "bring on line" the talents of your people to manage clearly-mandated activities under your overall guidance.

Does not the Bible compare the Church to a living body, of which Jesus is the head?  For anyone who's taken a high school course in biology, you know that the human body is composed of many interacting and overlapping processes comprising an overall smoothly-functioning system.

JESUS IS THE MIND CONTROLLING EVERYTHING. BUT MANY TASKS ARE "DELEGATED" TO THE VARIOUS PARTS OF THE CHURCH BODY.

Wise Godly Leadership acts out this New Testament example in the local congregation.

**Possible Action Items:**
- Consider if you and the rest of the leadership are finding adequate time to step back and *periodically assess the "big picture."*
- Discuss if there are duties that you and the others could readily *delegate direct involvement and/or management* to others?
- Institute *effective, ongoing training programs* to help people increase their skill levels to take over specified duties you've been handling yourself.
- Delegate authority to research and present to you-all *excellent options from Work Groups or committees* instead of trying to figure it all out yourselves.
- As the appointed, official leadership you cannot delegate authority to make the final decisions: but there's nothing in the Bible forbidding you to *establish management structures* under your oversight and control, not necessarily directly run by an Elder or a Deacon.

. . . . . . . . . . . . . . . . . . . . . . . . . . . . . . . . . . . . . . . . . . . . . . . . . . . . . . . . . . . .

44) **Change your Leadership Mandate from "protect the Truth" to "*help your people* to DO the Truth"** --- JESUS WAS NOT A PREACHER SPOUTING VAGUE GENERALITIES DEFENDING TRADITION, BUT A TRUE LEADER WHO DEMONSTRATED BY HIS OWN ACTIONS HOW TO MOVE FORWARD IMPLEMENTING RADICAL PRINCIPLES.

Yes, I know I've already mentioned this concept a number of times in previous points. But it needs to be a point of its own in this section on "Leadership."

Many Church of Christ leaders (preachers, elders, deacons) see their main job as: "Protect the Truth!" Indeed, many other religious groups do the same. However, this was not what Jesus did! If Jesus, an extremely-talented student of righteousness, had seen this as his job, he would have remained meekly in the synagogue studying the existing scriptures---not gathering thousands to him on the mountaintops to radically shake-up the foundations of the existing religion! Jesus stated his intent to "tear down the Temple" (the center of the Jewish religion of his time) and in three days build it up again in his own image!

Of course he was talking about his crucifixion then resurrection three days later: a death tied-into Christian baptism for "killing the old man of sin" and "rising to a new life in God!" This was not just "getting saved" but an entire *revitalization*---where a dead corpse returns to life!

JESUS WAS NOT ABOUT COMPLACENT STAGNATION BUT REGENERATION!

Yet the actions of many Church of Christ congregations teach that the best thing a member can do is sit motionless, silently, on a pew at a church service! Yes, the wordage of the sermons and lectures sometimes says differently. But when almost all the "church time" of the members is used sitting on pews, the actions say differently---to members, their children, and their community!

If people in the community are even aware of that "church there on the corner" it's of a group of people who sit on pews with their noses stuck in a song book or in a Bible---not a group of active, energized disciples of Jesus!

A person who studies the Bible quickly figures out its "take-home messages." Sure a person could spend all of his or her life becoming a scholar in every little detail in the Bible, that's true. But the main things of the Bible are fairly clear, easy to understand, and don't require going over and over them to the exclusion of putting them collectively into practice!

Why should we emphasize "collectivity"? Because *we each individually don't have all necessary talents to do everything*! We need to work together as a true body---where each of the parts supports all the rest of the parts! This is clear Bible instruction! Yet Church of Christ congregations spend almost all of their time lecturing individual Christians on going out and individually doing everything!

Sure, this type of sermonizing is easy. It's just making a speech. It's just vibrating air molecules. Figuring out how to find "church time" for people to actually work together, then put in place the mechanisms (such as work teams, small-group fellowship meetings, and mutual-interest talent facilitation) actually doing the Radical Principles of Jesus...is hard! Facilitating the talents of your people to work effectively together is a real challenge!

Instead of taking the easy way out haranguing your people for not individually doing the work of the Lord, figure out good mechanisms that actually help them pool their talents enjoyably together! *Other* religious groups are able to do this! It *is* possible! Take on the larger duty as your main job! Set your AIM high!

Determine your success not by how hard you preach but by the real results your congregation together produces. *Let this be the judge of your leadership: not just Faith, but Faith made manifest in Action*!

**Possible Action Items:**
- *Study together books* on how to effectively manage, mobilize, and empower a nonprofit, volunteer organization in today's society.
- *Bring in an outside consultant* --- who can give you a broad perspective across different organizations on techniques and methods possibly useful to you for motivating productive action.
- *Study the actions of Jesus* --- as the Ultimate Example on how to implement Jesus' Radical Principles.
- Consider how you might in the present-day society *emulate the actions of Jesus.*
- Include in each sermon, each lecture, and each Bible class *an action component.*
- *In small-group home studies* require a major activity each quarter in which everyone participates implementing the things they've been studying.
- *Change the main instruction of youth classes* from "study" to "application."
- *Change evangelistic efforts* from studying doctrine to involvement in congregational programs that demonstrate Jesus in action.
- *Emphasize sermons giving real examples* of people today together putting the Radical Principles of Jesus into action; for general inspiration or actual involvement of people in the audience!

---

## Chapter Seven:

# CRISIS MANAGEMENT

45) **When challenged by adverse circumstances, instead of falling back on accepted practices, attitudes, and beliefs which may or may not work, look first to Jesus and ask:** *"How can we do what Jesus already demonstrated to us?"* --- JESUS' FOOTSTEPS WERE NOT GLOWING WITH SUNSHINE BUT COATED IN HIS OWN BLOOD!

Church of Christ congregations---just like every other religious group---are very susceptible *to doctrinal fracturing*. "Doctrinal fracturing" is my term for when tradition diverges, with two different options dividing a previously-united congregation. This often happens because of unconscious ego-dominance on an issue.

The classic example of a trivial religious issue that can readily divide groups is: "How many angels can dance on the head of a pin?" This issue has little or no importance to living a Godly life. However, once brought up it can become an issue around which people stake out their positions; attach their egos, fight, and divide!

Think back to the issues that divided a congregation of which you were a part. Were they "life-and-death" matters upon which your salvation hung? Probably they were not. Likely they were some fairly trivial questions upon which people unconsciously hung their egos: such that the dispute wasn't in accepting or rejecting some position, but you not accepting *me*! Yes, this is not unique to religious organizations. Business, politics, other nonprofits---even your own family---are subject to ego-creep in which the issue at hand is supplanted by your ego!

Most of the religious fights that have resulted in tradition-divergence resulting in different churches are over trivial issues not necessary to salvation! That's the sad truth. But since these matters *are* often not essential to salvation, then there is hope for resolution if the ego-dominance can be overcome!

How does this happen? It happens when you have Wise Godly Leadership putting Quality (well-meeting the agreed-on AIM, Goals, and Objectives) over personal pride! Yet JESUS SUBMITTED TO GOD AND TO US IN ACCEPTING THE ULTIMATE PENALTY (SEPARATION FROM GOD ON THE CROSS) WHEN HE WAS ENTIRELY IN THE RIGHT!

And too often the church Leadership is the very worst example at acting *not* like Jesus but like mere little prideful, angry, squabbling children! "I'm right!" "No, *I'm* right!" become the battle-cries of the supposed Leaders.

*Wise Godly Leadership does not allow potential issues to become ego-suckers that end up polarizing the membership resulting in a "split"*! They step in at an early stage to diffuse and hopefully resolve the issue before it becomes a "You or Me" insurmountable problem! But, having failed to do so, trying to "crisis-manage" a situation is far more difficult than successfully nipping the problem in the bud.

Just remember that in a crisis is where your Wise Godly Leadership is tested! Will you admit your failure to avoid the crisis in the first place? Will you accept blame? Will you divert the tension away from the congregation and upon yourself? And then will you---if it's possible---find some novel way to resolve the situation while soothing both sides of the damaged ego-clumps?

Obviously the existing traditional mechanisms did not work, or you'd not be where you are in the middle of a huge fight! You've got to reach beyond what you already know! Can you do it? Instead of getting enough votes on your side so you can "win" and the others will "lose," can you instead bring people back together?

JESUS ALLOWED HIMSELF TO BE CRUCIFIED SO THAT SINNERS WOULD LOOK UP TO HIM HANGING IN AGONY BETWEEN HEAVEN AND EARTH---AND BY HIS SACRIFICE BE RECONCILED BOTH TO EACH OTHER AND TO GOD! Yes, this is a radically different attitude and operational imperative than: "I'm right and you're wrong!"

Is the ruling imperative to "purge" your congregation of people who don't accept every aspect of the prevailing tradition? Then, by all means, kick out the "misbelievers"! Of course don't be surprised when you end up with a congregation of "1" (yourself), since no one believes exactly the same as everyone else on everything!

But if the management objective to help your membership put first-things first, to grow rather than shrink the congregation, and to attract and inspire visitors/youth/members---then find good solutions! Yes, it may be very confusing, difficult, and even humiliating to not just fight to get *your* way...but it may help to save your congregation!

I well remember when a preacher suddenly resigned at a small congregation of which I was one of the leaders. In announcing his sudden departure I made some uncharitable observations as to his motivations, even though I felt it was necessary for the congregation to understand the situation in order to move forward. Unfortunately, my words made the situation far worse---threatening to split the congregation between those sympathetic to the departed minister and those who agreed that *he* was at fault!

So the very next Sunday morning service I went forward at the invitation and confessed sin, asking for the prayers of the congregation for forgiveness: reading-aloud a short apology and statement that I'd already gotten approved (after some revisions) by the departed preacher. It instantly defused the situation, even though I was personally humiliated.

That's the only time I've ever gone forward to admit personal sin---in a situation where I honestly felt I was not at fault and had done nothing wrong! Now I'm no martyr, but when that unexpected crisis arose I had to choose between my own ego and Jesus. Fortunately, I somehow found the strength to put Jesus first.

**Possible Action Items:**
- Reasonably *discuss "issues" privately* with the parties concerned BEFORE a crisis arises!
- *Have a back-up leadership-advisement platform* in place BEFORE it should be needed in unexpected crises!
- *Resist the urge to take a "right" side* and instead try to remain neutral: patiently listening to the full arguments from each side of the issue.
- *Put the ultimate good of the congregation before even being "right"*: completely aware of the real consequences that will unfold in response to any leadership decision you might make!
- *Be willing to be "wrong" if it will help your congregation* --- doing as Paul said and did: "willing to become all things to all people if it would win some to Christ."
- *Bring in an outside consultant* --- who can give clear-headed advice and new options for better-handling the crisis.
- *Verbally ask your fellow church leaders*: "What would Jesus do in this situation?"

. . . . . . . . . . . . . . . . . . . . . . . . . . . . . . . . . . . . . . . . . . . . . . . . . . . . . . . .

46) **Don't allow yourselves to take the safe, simple, and easy "way out"** --- JESUS RAILED AGAINST DOCTRINES OF MEN SUPPLANTING AND KILLING THE RADICAL PRINCIPLES OF TRUE GODLINESS.

What is the "easy" way out? Very simply, it is "No!" or "Go!"---"I'm right, you're wrong!" "Do it my way or leave!" "You don't like it, there's the door!"

Wise Godly Leadership is willing to work to try to understand the true motivations and reasoning of sincere people who are disagreeing with each other! *Furthermore, Quality Management seeks "win-win" solutions where everyone benefits---instead of "win-lose" or "lose-lose" situations where an individual or group is humiliated and disenfranchised!*

You've probably heard about "win-win" solutions and may have dismissed the whole idea as impractical, even evil! Yes, there are many folks out there who see any "compromise" as inherently evil! "The Truth is the Truth and you can't compromise on it!" But in matters not essential to salvation, there's a lot of room for good solutions that satisfy the valid spiritual needs of people on opposite sides of an argument!

Yes, getting to a "win-win" solution is often difficult, time-consuming, and tricky. It is not the "easy" way out of a crisis. Every instinct in the stressed-out leadership screams: "Stop this painful situation!"---telling you to take the easy, quick, and "clean" way out! Just quiet the critical, "evil" people by cutting them off, shutting them up, or kicking them out!

But to seriously consider their position, you must take the time and empathy necessary to help *them* to uncover *their* hidden assumptions behind their position---then look for shared *values* upon which a "win-win" solution can be constructed!

Once again, this whole process is complicated, difficult, and even dangerous! Indeed, success in this exploration may require bringing in a trained, expert Negotiator---or learning those skills oneself! Of course that has its own problems: 1) the idea that any negotiation is unacceptable "compromise"; 2) admission that the leadership is not perfect and needs help; and 3) fear at admitting failure to manage competing ideas in a healthy manner. So there are very strong forces at work to push the "easy" way out!

Let me give you another example. As congregations grow, various factions normally form. If the Leadership is not on top of those factions, creating viable management structures, providing healthy communication mechanisms, the competing ideas can quickly become issues that morph into ego-driven crises.

A common crisis in Church of Christ congregations involves concerned parents realizing that the "status quo" is not only *not* inspiring their children, but actually "turning them off" to church! In desperation, they search for some way to interest their children in being at church: which runs directly into the conservative Church of Christ notion that the church is a school and not a play-yard!

Yes, we're back again to the Church of Christ self-identification as "intellects" of the Christian world. From this perspective, kids should be taught to sit quietly during long, boring adult-level sermons and lectures, go to Bible "class" to memorize verses and survey the Old Testament, and spend their home time sitting dutifully reading the Bible.

The "liberal" parents would like a time and place for their children to enjoy good, productive fellowship with fellow Christian young-people! From this reasonable idea comes the notion to build a "gymnasium" for all sorts of fun sports to be done in a Christian environment. But the idea of putting out money for anything except self-comfort items (comfortable preacher, comfortable worship/class building, and comforting overseas evangelism program) often enrages the conservative factions! "How dare these liberals want to turn the church into a sports-program! That's not what church is supposed to be!"

I ran into this same cement-wall of opposition when I set up a ping pong table in a storage room for use by the kids (and me) after church services! After during our "duty" properly sitting silent and still for the required sermon, lectures, and Bible classes---me and some of the young people would have a few minutes of good Christian fun after the services! But not only was this not supported by the leadership, it was killed. Without asking me about it, the ping pong table was dismantled and thrown away. Nope, "ping pong" was just *not* appropriate for a church building!

A worst example of that was another congregation that wanted to build a gymnasium, costing lots of money! The end of the fight was the "liberals" departing the congregation, leaving behind a small remnant "conservative" faction. Is there a verse in the Bible that prohibits children from having fun at church? Is there a passage that forbids ping pong after services? By any stretch of the imagination, is hanging a basketball net up on a church outside wall for use by kids (and some adults!) after the services going to cause a person to go to hell? Not likely! But when it violates "sanctified" traditional beliefs and practices, it is as if Satan were being directly invited to come and join the congregation!

The easy answer is: "No, we don't do that!" The safe "solution" is: "We don't have the money!" The simple directive is: "If you don't like it, go elsewhere!" Once again, the whole conflict falls back on "right" or "wrong" answers, instead of Wise Godly Leaders working to discover valid spiritual needs, search for novel solutions to meet those needs, and bring competing people together instead of driving them further apart.

What might have been a Wise Godly Leadership-decision in that situation? Since the congregation was bulging at the seams in a small building, why not consider constructing a "multi-use" additional building? With easily-moved partitions, a large space could easily be used for more classrooms, more fellowship areas, and (when the partitions are all moved back) a large space for all sorts of enjoyable, fellowship-stimulating, young-and-older-people activities!

That's just one "win-win" possibility. How about renting the local high school gymnasium occasionally for church-sponsored young people (and older people) sports events? How about joining together with another church in the community to tap-into existing young people activity programs that they already have up and running? How about striking to the heart of the problem, a lack of meaningful young people fellowship, and looking for good alternatives for close productive fellowship other than having to gear up some complicated sports program?

Yes, all these options are complicated, difficult, and even a bit dangerous rather than just saying: "No!" All your human and leadership instincts are screaming out for you to reject them out-of-hand---and fall back to easy solutions! As Wise Godly Leadership you need to deliberately and consciously refuse to accept the potentially-disastrous, seemingly "easy," "simple," and "safe" way out! Instead, take the "Jesus" way out!

**Possible Action Items:**
- In any crisis, pause and take time to *list all the potential consequences* (immediately, long-term, and eternally) for all possible leadership decisions.
- *Ask the participants on each side of the crisis to come up with their own possible win-win" solutions* that take into account the valid spiritual needs of the people on the opposite side of the argument.

- *Bring in an outside consultant* who is expert in helping opposing sides find common values upon which to build viable "win-win" solutions.
- *Work to facilitate* the constructive expression of the talents of your membership meshing nicely together.
- *Study Books together* in advance of any crisis: on the tools, techniques, and strategies for healthy crisis management.

. . . . . . . . . . . . . . . . . . . . . . . . . . . . . . . . . . . . . . . . . . . . . . . . . . . . . . .

47) **Look for "win-win" solutions instead of "right or wrong" fights** --- JESUS LOOKED TO HELP PEOPLE MOVE CLOSER TO GOD RATHER THAN CONDEMN THEM FOR THEIR EVER-PRESENT FAULTS!

Yes, I've already talked about this. But it needs to be its own discrete point! Your Leadership *attitude* in approaching a crisis---not just your immediate management skills---will determine the outcome!

What "attitude" on the part of the leadership is best? Well, why not strive to have the attitude of *Jesus*?! In a crisis, we naturally---as fear-driven, survival-striving humans---fall back on the basest of emotions. Should not Church Leaders strive to be better than just squabbling fighters?

This "fall back" attitude of defensiveness is particularly strong in religion: where Tradition often trumps all else. From the reactions of Church leaders in various crisis situations, it often seems that "being Right" is far more important than finding good solutions.

Church Leaders often seem more happy that their entire congregation has been split down the middle ("getting rid of" supposed evil heretics) than crying over the fact that their congregation has in one fell swoop been crippled! What are these church leaders thinking? Don't they realize that it will take years to recover from this crippling blow, if ever?

"Fighting for the Right" does not mean horrifying your membership, shocking your children, and driving away visitors! People do not come to church in order to wage ideological wars over things not essential to salvation! They come for reassurance, for inspiration, for close Godly fellowship, and to be part of morally-meaningful service!

You can still be *entirely wrong*---even when you are technically "in-the-right"! In other words, you can absolutely and totally lose the war as you gloat over winning some small battle! If only those who believe the "right" things are allowed in your congregation then you might as well reconcile yourself to having a "congregation" with only one member, you! No one believes exactly the same on everything!

But JESUS WAS NOT ABOUT FORCING EVERYONE INTO THE SAME TRADITION, RATHER IN UNITING PEOPLE ON A COMMON GOAL: OPENING OUR HEARTS EVER MORE FULLY TO GOD!

Instead of giving the people yet another "officially-sanctified" number for how many steps they could walk on the Sabbath and not violate the Law of Moses, JESUS CHALLENGED THE PEOPLE WITH THE GREATEST TASK OF ALL: TRULY LOVING GOD WITH ALL OUR HEARTS, MINDS AND SOULS!

When Godly Wise Leadership works hard to promote and keep people focused on an agreed-upon *AIM* (at the center of one's Vision)---and making sure that the congregation's long-term Goals and shorter-term Objectives align with that AIM---then trivial disputes and disagreements pale to insignificance.

Instead of "I think this way is best" the discussion becomes "How can we all contribute our good talents together to accomplish the *AIM*/Goal/Objective?" It's a different "mindset": that of Jesus. It's truly "submitting" not just to arbitrary, handed-down, imposed "solutions"---but to the highest Radical Principles of our Lord.

**Possible Action Items:**
- *Cultivate an attitude of listening* --- allowing the other person(s) ample time to make their points before disrespectfully interrupting and cutting them off.

- Without giving up your responsibility as an appointed Leader to make the final decision, *solicit a variety of good options* to any problem or opportunity.
- *Don't think that you have to come up with all the solutions* --- recognizing your incomplete knowledge or talents in any situation; keeping the appropriate people "in the loop" rather than excluding or ignoring the valid spiritual needs of disagreeing factions.
- *"Thank" people for their suggestions* --- even when those suggestions are obviously unworkable, ignorant, or bad!
- *Study books* on helpful conflict resolution, on building flexible management structures, and on facilitation techniques/methods.
- *Recognize that while fighting is bad, intelligent give-and-take is a good use of your time*---but takes both sides to do this, both them <u>and</u> you!
- Instead of asking for a committee to come up with "a" solution --- instead give them the mandate for *providing at least three different solutions complete with potential positives and negatives for each situation.*
- *Put in place the necessary training and ongoing support* that's required for any program or congregational effort to stay on track.
- *Provide trained Facilitators* --- for use in Work Groups, Small-group Home Studies, meetings, or classes: who are expert in maintaining a healthy "people process" in people-on-people situations where friction is inevitable.

. . . . . . . . . . . . . . . . . . . . . . . . . . . . . . . . . . . . . . . . . . . . . . . . . . .

48) **Truly demonstrate love to all** --- JESUS SAID HIS FOLLOWERS WERE REQUIRED TO TRULY LOVE BY THEIR ACTIONS NOT ONLY THEIR NEIGHBORS BUT EVEN THEIR ACTUAL, LETHAL ENEMIES!

Sometimes Christian people and groups express a greater *HATE* towards each other than to their worst enemies! This irrational, non-Christ-like hate is justified by "hating sin not the sinner"---where the sinner in actuality is belittled, excluded, and figuratively (or literally) killed! This is the notion: "I love you so much that I'm willing to kill you if you don't believe and say what I say God wants you to believe and say!"

Uh huh...well, with that kind of "love" who needs enemies? This is not what Jesus taught---neither by his words or actions! JESUS EXPLICITLY STATED THAT WE ARE TO LOVE EVEN OUR ENEMIES TO THE POINT OF EXPRESSING IT BEING HELPFUL TO THEM IN WAYS THAT THEY WOULD AGREE ARE HELPFUL! Jesus required us to do this to our *ENEMIES*---those actively trying to harass, torture, and kill us!

This is one of those Radical Principles that many Christians today love to pretend don't exist! But are we just regular humans loving those who are nice to us while despising and fighting against those that don't? Do we only have a thin veneer of "religiosity" to disguise us being just smart animals? Or do we truly believe what we preach?

Against those who are mean to us, who don't agree with our politics, who fail to be nice to us, who don't echo our traditional beliefs and practices: is it ok to demonize and attack them? No! JESUS SAID WHEN WE ARE SLAPPED ON THE FACE, TO TURN OUR OTHER CHEEK FOR ANOTHER SLAP RATHER THAN DEMAND "A TOOTH FOR A TOOTH"!

Did Jesus not say this? Is this not another of those Radical Principles that Christians love to pretend don't exist? Furthermore, did not JESUS REQUIRE US HIS FOLLOWERS TO BEHAVE TOWARDS OTHERS AS WE'D WANT THEM TO BEHAVE TOWARDS US? Is this not yet another of those inconvenient, difficult, complicated, and dangerous Radical Principles that many Christians love to pretend doesn't exist?

Is your #1 duty as a Church Leader to defend doctrine against attack or to show your love to even your hard-core Enemies by your tangible actions? DID NOT JESUS IN HIS GREATEST CRISIS DEMONSTRATE BY HIS ACTIONS DIVINE LOVE: VOLUNTARILY SACRIFICING HIMSELF TAKING UPON HIMSELF THE PUNISHMENT FOR THE SINS OF THOSE WHO WERE STILL SINNERS?

Are any crises that you face in your congregation equal to the crisis Jesus faced when most of his followers deserted him, his Religious Leadership condemned him, and he faced crucifixion by the Roman soldiers?

AND YET IN ALL THIS, JESUS---WHILE HANGING IN AGONY ON THE CROSS---WAS STILL ABLE TO CROAK OUT THESE WORDS TO GOD: "FORGIVE THEM, FATHER...THEY KNOW NOT WHAT THEY DO!" Is this your attitude to so-called "liberals" or traditional "heretics" who argue for slight changes to help your children, members, and visitors be drawn closer to God?

Yes, they may be wrong. But are they wrong out of malice or displaced enthusiasm? Can you not consider their positive motivations, even if they are in error? *Can you not work to find ways to better-meet their valid spiritual needs?*

If you can, then you are: 1) demonstrating Godly love; 2) meeting hurtful criticism with patient listening; and 3) behaving toward them as you'd have them behave toward you!

Demonstrate God's love not as a theory but as a fact. Pretend that you are Jesus!

**Possible Action Items:**
- *Request a meeting with your closest "splinter" Church of Christ congregation leaders* --- not to argue who's right or wrong on various doctrinal issues; but to see if there are good ways you might cooperate together in worthwhile activities for your young people, members, and community.
- *Request a meeting with the closest Christian group's leadership other than Church of Christ* --- not to argue who's right or wrong on various doctrinal issues; but to see if there are good ways you might cooperate together in worthwhile activities for your young people, members, and community.
- *Discuss and determine who your real "enemies" are; and find out what you can do for them that will be helpful to them in good ways that they deem are helpful* --- (imagine this approach for Jews versus Palestinians, or Christians versus Muslims, or any other groups locked in racial and historical bloody conflicts).
- *Find ways to help sinners* --- not just by criticizing and condemning them from afar; but by meeting some of their valid needs in ways that show them Jesus in action.
- *Thank people for their constructive criticisms by patiently listening to them* --- even if you deem them to be unworthy of you paying them any attention at all!
- *Help your people to accomplish goals that they deem worthy* --- putting out the effort and time to study and implement Quality Management and Facilitation.

. . . . . . . . . . . . . . . . . . . . . . . . . . . . . . . . . . . . . . . . . . . . . . . . . . . . .

49) **Stop making excuses blaming science, entertainment, or Satan for your own failures** --- JESUS SAID THAT ANYONE WHO WANTED TO BE HIS DISCIPLE HAD TO TAKE UP THEIR OWN CROSS AND FOLLOW IN HIS BLOOD-SOAKED FOOTSTEPS!

*The worst possible result of Church management and leadership is allowing a "split" to occur!*

When the congregation under your oversight is split down the middle, with half the group quitting or going elsewhere, this is the "dynamite" for church disintegration! It isn't just failing to keep some children, or failing to keep some visitors, or failing to stop a few members from sliding out the back door---it's *PUBLICLY PROCLAIMING A CATASTROPHIC FAILURE OF YOUR LEADERSHIP!*

No, it wasn't Satan that snuck in and snared half your congregation! No, it wasn't "liberals" who just "wanted to be entertained" that enticed-away half of your congregation! No, it wasn't "evolution, global warming, or the Hubble space-telescope" that conspired to undermine your teachings! It was a failure of your leadership.

You failed to recognize the valid spiritual needs of your congregation. You failed to provide good, appropriate "win-win" solutions to conflicts. You failed to mediate disputes and prevent them from turning into ego-driven crises in the first place! You failed. Ok. Let's just admit the truth.

In the leadership example I mentioned previously concerning myself, *I* failed---but didn't give up! Instead, I somehow found the strength (it was very hard!) to admit my failure, ask for forgiveness, and then keep on trying my best to exercise Godly Wise Leadership: *LEARNING FROM MY FAILURES HOW TO DO BETTER IN THE FUTURE!*

I did not continue in my failure. I did not "double-down" on how I was right and the others were wrong! I did not gloat how I had "won the fight" by endangering half the congregation, visitors, and the children's faith in God. Instead, I determined to try to understand what had happened, grow from the bad situation, and be a better servant of the Lord.

That personal management and leadership failure occurred to me a long time ago, long before I learned about Quality Management or had written any of my books on The Real Jesus, etc. At that time I still had a lot more to learn about effective Church management! But I'm still here---and still learning!

Unfortunately, the Church of Christ leadership is infamous for not learning. The Church of Christ is infamous for foisting its biggest failures (to keep its young people, inspire its members, keep visitors, and recruit new members) upon the "scapegoats" of Science, Entertainment, and Satan.

Preachers love to blame the membership or society for not jumping-up-and-down with enthusiasm at boring sermons repeating doctrinal arguments known and accepted by most everyone present.

Listen, my friends. If you cannot admit your personal failures---and the failures of the "Church of Christ" denomination---then you can never get better! You are doomed to get worse...and die-out!

Yes, the beginning of Wisdom is truly Humility: to not just accept without regard to its successfulness the prevailing traditional beliefs and practices---but to rise beyond them to the Radical Principles of Jesus!

It is difficult, uncertain, and even dangerous. But it is also tremendously empowering, exciting, and productive!

Yes, careless flaunting of Radical Principles can burn down the entire organization. Or---under the oversight of Godly Wise Leadership---they can be the "rocket-fuel" to launch us to unprecedented heights of success!

**Possible Action Items:**
- *Write a list of your personal leadership failures --- plus what you learned from each failure for doing better in the future.*
- *Write a list of where your congregation is presently failing --- plus which actions of Jesus might give clues as to how to overcome those failures.*
- *Write a list of your own possible Action Items on how your congregation's preaching might be improved --- to better-connect with visitors, inspire your members, and interest your young people.*
- *Write a list of your own possible Action Items on how your congregation's services might be improved --- to better-connect with visitors, inspire your members, and interest your young people.*
- *Write a list of your own possible Action Items on how your congregation's classes might be improved --- to better-connect with visitors, inspire your members, and interest your young people.*
- *Write a list of your own possible Action Items on how your congregation's youth program might be improved --- to better-connect with visitors, involve your members, and inspire your young people.*
- *Write a list of your own possible Action Items on how your congregation's local evangelism program might be improved --- to better-connect with visitors, involve more of your members, and bring in young people.*
- *Write a list of your own possible Action Items on how your congregation's benevolence program might be improved --- to better-connect with your community, inspire your members to participate, and give opportunity for service to your young people.*

- *Make your own list of the Radical Principles of Jesus --- and your own possible Action Items on how your congregation might do better at linking your talents together to carry them out.*

. . . . . . . . . . . . . . . . . . . . . . . . . . . . . . . . . . . . . . . . . . . . . . . . . . . . . . . .

50) **Put in the time** --- JESUS DID NOT SHIRK FROM OR SHORT-CHANGE WHATEVER TASK WAS PUT BEFORE HIM.

This is my last and most important point for saving the dying Church of Christ. *Every point already covered (all 49 of them) will fail if this point is not followed*! It is critical to everything else.

Unfortunately, the leadership of Church of Christ congregations typically violates this requirement---doing so routinely and without regret. Is it any wonder that the Church under their direction is failing to keep its children, its members, or its visitors?

The worst and most insidious example is when the Leadership does decide to try and improve the procedures. Typically this "improvement" is imposed-down upon the congregation from above, with little or no explanation, as a surprise! As an unintended result---no matter how worthwhile the effort---it is doomed to fail.

Not having put in the time to carefully explain the improvement, advertise it in advance, keep promoting it as it nears, test it out first as a time-or-people-limited "pilot," carefully improve it until it's functioning well, and then with strong support from within the congregation to roll it out to the full congregation---many in the congregation simply oppose it on principle as something "new".

Having a tradition of unquestioning submission, though, the congregation may grudgingly accept the improvement. However, in a few weeks or months those in opposition will kill the improvement, either by neglecting it or actively working against it.

Many of those in opposition, however, might have "held their powder" to see if it actually worked---observing the benefits to young people, the membership, and visitors---and accepted it...if only the time had been put in to carefully and respectfully prepare the congregation and optimize the procedure before full implementation! But since the time *wasn't* put in, the improvement *fails.*

Anyone suggesting further improvements is then chastised with "we tried something similar in the past and it was a miserable failure!" So not only does not putting in the time doom the immediate improvement, it ripples into the future as a huge "wet blanket" on the enthusiasm of other would-be helpful suggestions.

Failing to put in the needed time to properly implement and support good improvements directly derives from the Elders and Deacons typically seeing their job as an obligation of a few hours a month.

Preachers/Ministers are also under huge time-constraints in that they are typically paid part-time, low pay for which the mandatory sermon and class preparation takes up most of their week.

A similar problem occurs with the membership that heroically spends up to four time-periods per week accomplishing little or nothing other than sitting listening to sermons and lectures on subjects they already know. Time is misused. Time is wasted. Time is constrained. Time is lost.

If the Elders and Deacons wish to take the main direct management responsibilities upon themselves then they need to also realize they must devote sufficient time to the necessary Leadership functions! A brief meeting once per month isn't enough.

The problem with misspent or constrained time also extends down to the monthly Men's Business Meeting. If it wants to wrestle with the true spiritual problems holding back the church (other than fixing leaks in the roof), then a brief hour is not enough!

If preachers want to connect with their young people, members, and visitors in a meaningful way then spending most of their paid time grinding out doctrinal lectures isn't a sufficient use of their time!

If members want to be inspired with carefully-managed close fellowship, have their talents synergize with other people's attempting great works, and be inspired to greater Godliness---then allowing their "church time" to be burned up passively listening to boring lectures and "Mickey-Mouse" style Bible classes won't work!

Leadership needs to study, discuss, and implement effective Jesus-derived methods and techniques of Godly Quality Management. This takes time. It takes setting aside a regular, relaxed, non-rushed period of time each month to study, discuss, and grow together where regular "business" is banned!

Preachers need their sermon/lecture/class requirements to be drastically decreased (by the Eldership bringing in expert speakers on targeted subjects) in order to be more involved in facilitation, organization, and training of others!

Members need some of their required "church time" to be opened-up for facilitated, well-supported close fellowship and synergistic joyful service.

Young people need to be given a significant budget so that a well-organized committee of them, parents, and others can put in the time and effort to plan and implement highly-impactful quarterly activities that enthuse and inspire!

Women need the overt support and encouragement by the men to spend the time to organize and self-manage their own excellent synergistic efforts that will end up saving the church!

No, it's not "preaching harder and longer" or "instituting yet another duplicate worship service" or "requiring mandated make-work" or "sticking into the weekly schedule a lady's study class" on top of everything else! It's working smarter, not just working longer!

In fact, the "church" time people put-out may actually decrease! The church activities don't necessarily lengthen, but go from diffuse time-wasters to being *focused*---with better, tighter, more-effective *AIM* & Goals & Objectives driving the agendas.

JESUS DID NOT JUST "DO" THINGS OR WASTE TIME! IN A SHORT LIFE OF 33 YEARS HE CHANGED THE FACE OF RELIGION AND BROUGHT MANKIND CLOSER TO GOD!

In like fashion, the Church of Christ needs to put Jesus first---even *more* important than traditional beliefs and practices---by not just plodding through yet another ritualistic service, but by spending the time doing whatever is necessary to actually move its children, members, and visitors closer to God!

**Possible Action Items:**
- *Put in the time to properly "roll-out" any agreed-on improvements* to the church schedule or activities, being careful to do the following: 1) fully explain by mail-outs and announcements the value of this to the congregation, requesting feedback; 2) take all questions, comments, and concerns seriously, patiently answering and incorporating good ideas wherever possible; 3) keep promoting the upcoming improvement, making it clear that it is a "pilot test" limited in scope or time; 4) evaluate the piloted improvement

with real data for if it actually achieves the desired objective; 5) make improvements to the improvement, repeating the pilot if warranted; 6) re-evaluate, continuing to enhance and refine the improvement until it is functioning well; 7) only then "roll out" the improvement to the full congregation, with continued strong support and promotion from the leadership.
- *Elders, Deacons, and Minister(s) set aside a monthly meeting time to study Quality Management subjects*: a meeting that is not rushed, not for regular business, and relaxed --- its purpose is to ever-learn how to be ever-better at Godly Quality Leadership (constantly striving to be better at doing their job for Jesus and God).
- *The time is put in to prepare difficult sermons presenting scriptures mainly in the up-front context of addressing real problems* of the members of the congregation & community rather than just defending traditional "milk"-level doctrines (offering real Biblical insights into difficult specific problems; to which members would feel comfortable bringing their friends and neighbors).
- *Carefully design impactful, interesting, joyful church services* --- instead of rote-repetition, boring, rituals (with the goal of actual edification and inspiration of intelligent members rather than treating the members like stupid children needing endless repetition).
- Instead of having a duplicate Sunday-evening worship service --- *use Sunday evening for small-group home meetings* where interesting, meaningful, Questions to the morning sermon are discussed; and to which members feel comfortable inviting their friends and relatives (that's well-designed, well-supported, and well-run).
- Institute a *Friendship Evangelism program* that is well-funded, well-organized, and ongoing---that involves a wide range of talented members in a variety

of necessary roles (which is strongly promoted and supported by the appointed leadership).
- Fund a strong *Youth Fellowship/Service Quarterly Activity* --- by setting aside into a special fund the first 10% of all offerings: administered by a committee that meets regularly, involving key young people, parents, teachers, and other interested individuals (where any plans they make are studied and approved by the appointed leadership).
- Use a *midweek meeting time for overt Work Groups* that are well-facilitated to allow smooth interaction of members (both adults and children) that well-utilize their talents and interests (moving the Radical Principles of Jesus from discussion to implementation).
- *Expand the monthly Men's Business Meeting* to several hours, allowing sufficient time each month to address not just maintenance (like fixing the leaking roof) but the true spiritual priorities of managing the various fellowship and work groups' focused efforts (helping the appointed leadership by doing a lot of the spiritual "grunt-work").
- *Allow and encourage a Women's Work Monthly Meeting* in parallel to the Men's (as commissioned, sanctioned, and overseen by the appointed leadership).
- *Appointed Leadership becomes more strategic* rather than tactical as success takes hold and the congregation starts retaining its youth, energizing its members, and attracting visitors.

----------

# **Conclusion:**

The dying Church of Christ can be saved. But it will require Godly Wise Leadership putting Jesus before Tradition. Unfortunately, this will be very difficult. People love their religious traditions, whether or not they accomplish any desirable objective.

When the Catholic Church stopped having their services in Latin---a language most of the people did not understand---many rebelled! For them, "church" was listening to a mysterious but beautiful unknown language!

In similar fashion today, the shape of the pews, the timing of the procedures, the clothes worn, the songs sung, the way that doctrines are taught, and all other features of "doing church" quickly become set parts of cherished rituals.

But JESUS CAME TO BREAK MANKIND OUT OF THEIR CHERISHED RITUALS, CEREMONIES, AND BELIEFS. For Jesus, his *AIM* was clear: to *help mankind move closer to God*---teaching them Godliness not just by words but mainly through loving service to even those who did not deserve such kindness.

You as a Church of Christ member, whether part of the appointed leadership or not, can choose to adopt the *AIM* of Jesus! This radical *AIM* clearly implies that we are not perfect! That's the sad negative. But there's also a hopeful positive: that we have much room for improvement!

There is always going to be a distance between us and God. But the good news is that Jesus has given mankind the tools to shrink that gap! This radical Christian viewpoint applies not just to our personal righteousness but also to *everything* else! There is room for improvement in our beliefs, our doctrines, our procedures, our rituals, our weekly schedule, and our ceremonies---not by an increasingly-narrowing search for what is "right", but for better-applying the Radical Principles of Jesus!

Yes, actually implementing this *AIM* of Jesus is complicated, difficult, and even at times dangerous. It is far more comfortable to just accept the status quo as being supposedly sanctified by God, while demonizing anyone who suggests anything that's in any way different. I have no doubt that this short book---even though it's replete with many specific respectfully-helpful suggestions---will be condemned in sermons and banned from many Church of Christ congregations.

However, it is my hope that many good-hearted, courageous members and leaders of the Church of Christ will acknowledge their own short-comings and choose to truly put following Jesus as their #1 religious goal, above all else.

\* \* \* \* \* \* \* \* \* \* \* \* \* \* \* \* \* \* \* \* \* \* \* \* \* \* \* \* \* \* \* \* \* \* \*

# About the Author:

Daniel B. Lyle holds a Ph.D. in Biology, has successfully completed a more than forty-year research career in various university and governmental agency situations, and is the author of more than thirty books. He was raised in a mainline Church of Christ congregation and has been a faithful member of that group for many years. His books, free videos, and other services are available at his websites: [LylePublishing.com](LylePublishing.com) and [Creative-Theology.org](Creative-Theology.org).

\* \* \* \* \* \* \* \* \* \* \* \* \* \* \* \* \* \* \* \* \* \* \* \* \* \* \* \* \* \* \* \* \* \* \* \*

## Other Books by Dr. Lyle:

**The Book of Lyle**: a Spiritual Adventure from our Beginning to Beyond Death

**Creative-Theology®**: Definitions and implementation.

**In Search of Quality**: Principles & Mechanisms

**The God Debate**: Intelligent arguments about the idea of God.

**The Real Jesus**: A Creative-Theologist worthy of being followed.

**The Jesus Lectures 1**: How to find the Kingdom of God.

**The Jesus Lectures 2**: How to understand one's own heart.

**The Jesus Lectures 3**: How to deal with difficult people.

**The Jesus Lectures 4**: How to best express Godly Love.

**The Jesus Lectures 5**: How to master true Compassion

**The Jesus Lectures 6**: How to capitalize on Connectivity.

**The Jesus Lectures 7**: How to best understand God.

**The Jesus Lectures 8**: How to make your life Significant.

**The Jesus Lectures 9**: How to enjoyably avoid Damnation.

**The Jesus Lectures 10**: How to learn to cherish true Salvation.

* * * * * * * * * * * * * * * * * * * * * * * * * * * * * *

www.ingramcontent.com/pod-product-compliance
Lightning Source LLC
Chambersburg PA
CBHW060825050426
42453CB00008B/587